BRITAIN'S MOST ECCENTRIC SPORTS

RICHARD O. SMITH

First published 2012

The History Press
The Mill, Brimscombe Port
Stroud, Gloucestershire, GL5 2QG
www.thehistorypress.co.uk

British Library Cataloguing in Publication Data.
A catalogue record for this book is available from the British Library.

ISBN 978 0 7524 6413 8

Typesetting and origination by The History Press
Printed in India

About the Author

RICHARD O. SMITH writes the humorous *Oxford Examined* column for the *Oxford Times* magazine *Limited Edition* and writes for BBC Radio 4's topical comedies *The Now Show* and *The News Quiz*. His previous book *Oxford Student Pranks: A History of Mischief & Mayhem,* documenting competing debauchery between students, was published in 2010; author, broadcaster and rising history star Lucy Worsley described it as, 'I was expecting *Oxford Student Pranks* to be a jape-filled jamboree of jollity, but it turned out to be full of sex and violence as well. All human life is here, served up with a light touch and keen sense of the ridiculous.'

Previously Richard won the National Football Writer of the Year Award, edited the football fanzine *From Behind Your Fences* and wrote for various newspapers, magazines and comedians.

He presents the Eccentric Oxford Walking Tour: details at www.oxfordwalks.co.uk.

Foreword

So, you Britishers think you can challenge Germany's sporting supremacy by inventing eccentric new sports, and resurrecting some very old ones? Just put up your hands and surrender to German sporting domination, and stick to what you're really good at: which appears to be writing witty, fascinating and genuinely hilarious books about Britain's most eccentric sports. A wunderbar book. An ideal read for, say, a long spell in the cooler, or attending all 26 days of a cricket match.

Henning Wehn, comedian & German Comedy Ambassador

Introduction

Dedicating a book can cause surprising problems. Should it be dedicated to a parent, a spouse, or cash in on celebrity association ('to my biggest fan Nelson Mandela who said I made him feel humble')? Perhaps not the last one.

Luckily, the more books one writes, the more dedication potentials. So, parents = done (with no noticeable rise in pocket money – though, to be fair, they did point out I was forty-seven and that the Chancellor almost certainly intends to close the pocket money tax loophole in the next Budget). Wife = done. Which enables this book to be dedicated to another wholly worthy group of dedicees (I know that's not an actual noun, but hey, we're supposed to be celebrating quirky creative individualism here).

So this book is NOT dedicated to you, rejectionist Olympics, with your stand-offish, sniffy exclusivity, because you're only picking the sports the rest of the world is good at. Take a bow, eccentric sportsmen and sportswomen of Britain as this book is dedicated to you. You are the ones stepping up to the plate, line, crease, mark, oche and, less frequently, the podium, of eccentric sporting events. You're the ones dipping your dwile, chasing your cheese, hurling your rejected snack, launching your bathtub, riding your pram, racing your lawnmower, setting alight your tar barrel, jumping off your pier and dialling 999 when it all goes predictably wrong. Hence this book is dedicated with genuine respect to the participants, organisers and volunteers who ensure the continued existence of the wonderful Britain-enriching sports featured in this book.

This book intends to celebrate our most gloriously idiosyncratic and quintessentially British pastimes. While researching the book I met pram racers with smiles broader than the average, well, pram. And a male netball Goal Attack who literally couldn't shoot for laughing – an affliction that a Premiership footballer is less prone to suffer, unless contemplating the incomprehensibility of what he's paid. Never confuse what you earn with what you're worth. Some sports in this book, forced to be involuntarily penurious, are funded with the change from a shoestring. The yeast that enables the dough of eccentricity to rise into Britain's truly worthwhile sporting bread and butter is the enthusiasm displayed by amateur participants. As Churchill, himself a celebrant of British eccentricity, once imparted with characteristic perspicuity, 'success is not final, failure is not fatal: it is the courage to continue that counts.'

Participants in these eccentric sports share a pulsating awareness that they're competing for fun rather than merely the accomplishment of sporting excellence. Isn't that an ideology you once had, Olympics – and then seriously misplaced? Now the modern Olympics is supposedly just about one winner of each event, and which sugary drink provider and fatty fast food peddler are the official partners celebrating athleticism; London's Olympic venue boasts the planet's largest McDonalds; that bleeping sound you're currently hearing is an irony alarm going off.

There's a loudly knocking reality, thus far uncomfortably ignored, that the Olympics is somewhat aloof and elitist, discriminating against sports it considers to be of lower stock or breeding. Inestimable numbers of Britains participate in cricket, netball and rugby, rather more than the number who actively pick up their foils to fence – but you won't see the first three at the Olympics. Nor Dwile Flonking.

Britain's Most Eccentric Sports features the sports that are collectively closer to the British psyche, created by those who dared to dream out loud. Here you can spot a visible enthusiasm unbleached by perpetual defeat, possessing a healthy perspicacity that all sport is ultimately pointless (and that includes you, so stop looking so smug football, rugby and cricket) – and therein lies, in its ultimate futility, a large aspect of sport's wonderful attraction, i.e. after all that invested passion, aggression and emotion, there's not really that much harm done. Sport matters most when it provides excitement, exercise, social cohesion, dedication in the face of setbacks, exhilaration and (the one most often forgotten) fun. Oh, and beating Germany at something. Anything. That's the true British sporting spirit. And well worth celebrating.

Alnwick Shrovetide Football

Although the Northumbrian climate in January is unremittingly bleak – the life expectancy of a polar bear here would be a few short hours before irreversible hyperthermia took its inevitable toll – several spectators are huddled together for warmth like penguins, greeting the traditional start of the annual Alnwick Shrovetide Football game by cheering.

The fields outside Alnwick Castle where the game takes place are often saturated, resulting in dispirited players seeing the ball they have just given an almighty hoof with a giant's energy, merely being propelled exactly 4ft forward across the boggy waterlogged turf; at times the game resembles a splashing water fight, and diffident players display concerns as to the depth of puddles ahead, worried that a flying winger's mesmeric run could avoid defenders' tackles, but not a 5ft sheer drop into a lagoon.

Unlike many eccentric British sports that dishonestly include 'football' in their name although their event fails to feature anything remotely approaching actual football (e.g. Royal Ashbourne Football, Uppies & Downies Football, Ba Football, Stoke City Football Club), the annual Alnwick Shrovetide Football possesses broadly recognisable character traits with

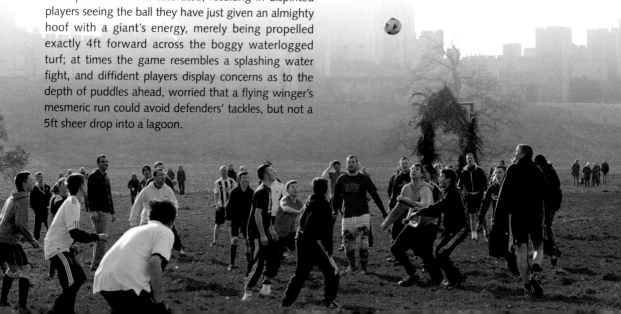

conventional football. Whereas several informal football games played casually over the years in the nation's streets and gardens have suddenly ceased whenever the ball sails through a window and everyone scarpers, inversely the Alnwick match traditionally commences when a ball sails out of a window. Specifically, a family member of the Duke of Northumberland is charged with starting each annual game, orchestrated by appearing at an upstairs window of Alnwick Castle while purposefully holding a ball – which must have led to misunderstandings during the planning stage:

Official: So, Duchess, the town will require you to hold a ball at the castle this year, and invite 100 guests.

Duchess: Superb. I've seen a wonderful ball gown and matching tiara I can wear, and we must hire a top band.

Official: Ah . . .

Commencing the 2011 game, Lord James, the brother of the duke, dutifully appeared at the castle window holding a football. Tradition decrees that he starts the game by lobbing the ball to the assembled players below, made up of 50 a side – which meant that both teams probably went for the tried and tested tactical 20-10-20 formation, with their overlapping five left backs and five right backs looking to get forward whenever possible.

Alnwick Shrovetide Football has traceable origins back to 1762, and is contested by the rival parishes of St Michael's and St Paul's. Consistent with many of Britain's eccentric sports, the game possesses its own terminology – and a goal is known as a 'hale'. Situated exactly quarter of a mile apart, hales are a recognisable set of wooden goalposts, though smaller and more rustic in manufacture than those familiar to the contemporary football watcher. Time keeping, like the playing surface itself, is uneven; the game is divided into three slots with each playing portion lasting for 20–30 minutes. However, once a hale has been scored, the game immediately discontinues until reconvening at the same place and time next year.

Dave Hubbard scored the deciding hale at the 2011 event, securing victory for the parish of St Paul's. With the game ended, the mud-splattered semi-swamp conditions of land surrounding Alnwick Castle ensures that players look like they're filming a washing powder advert. A traditional post-match dive into the adjacent River Aln was limited to two hardy, courageous – and presumably shivering until June – players.

The game has probably evolved from a more violent variant. Records show that the powerfully connected Henry de Ellington was killed during a football game in Northumbria in 1280, and soon several royal legates were issued denouncing the game, with no less than sixteen formal notices banning football following in the next 200 years. Thankfully, most were ignored.

Aunt Sally

o, not the character portrayed by Una Stubbs in *Worzel Gummidge*, but a rather idiosyncratically named eccentric British sport. Although enjoying continued popularity in Oxfordshire for at least two centuries, it now struggles to cross the county line although an occasional village residing just across the Buckinghamshire or Warwickshire border might

participate. The strongest theory for Aunt Sally's origins is contained within the egregious game Throwing At Cocks (you may want to skip reading the next bit – it's grisly).

In the sixteenth and seventeenth centuries, an unfortunate cockerel would be tied atop a wooden stake in a pub garden. Players would then hurl wooden blocks at the restrained cockerel, culminating in the thrower that killed the bird winning the bird. If the legs or wings were fractured, and they frequently were, then wooden sticks were attached to support the bird, permitting its suffering to continue. This was an era where Goose Pulling was also a popular sport – an unfortunate goose, with neck greased to decrease friction, would be suspended over a road while riders passing underneath attempted to pull off its head for a cash prize. The 'sport' Gänsereiten continues in Germany today as a Shrove Tuesday tradition – although legislation has decreed since 1920 that the goose must be killed prior to the repugnant contest (you have to say that's only a partial legal victory for the goose).

Progressive sensibilities ensured that live cockerels were eventually replaced with a doll, usually painted and sometimes clothed to resemble an ugly maid. By the nineteenth century, clay pipes were inserted into the dolls' mouths, with points scored for dislodging

These figures perhaps masquerade the impression of a healthy game, yet contrasting them to 15 years ago reveals that the number of divisions and teams has exactly halved.

Right, here's how the game is played in modern times. The eponymous Aunt Sally is a 6in wooden block known as a 'dolly'. Six wooden projectiles called 'sticks' measuring 18in each are then hurled at the dolly by sixteen players divided into two teams of eight. The dolly is positioned on a metre-high metallic spike – a kind of coconut shy holder. Players have three 'legs' to dislodge a dolly and must throw six sticks in each 'horse' (round). Games comprise three 'horses' where sticks must dislodge the dolly directly, yet not after hitting the spike first, wherein it's an illegal throw known as an 'iron'.

Missing a dolly with all eighteen throws is referred to as a 'blob', with offenders enduring the castigating noun 'blobbers'. A roll call of shame is traditionally printed in the local paper each week listing blobbers, and presumably debates how they can pick up the shattered remnants of their newly inadequate lives after such irreparable humiliation as they send an SAE to the Foreign Legion. The opposite of a blobber is a 'sixer' – the phrase reserved for a player who dislodges six dollies in one horse. Theoretically players can obtain three sixes in a match, dislodging a dolly with all eighteen throws – an occurrence that has been achieved on only fourteen occasions since the Oxfordshire leagues commenced in the 1930s.

them – something of an early zero-tolerance approach to smoking in pubs. As clay pipes fell out of fashion, so did the game's previous guise, and a modification to rules ensured the historic game spanned the twentieth century in a format currently recognisable to the twenty-first.

Oxford alone operates eleven divisions of ten teams, and boasts 1,376 registered players (being a predominately outdoor game, the season traditionally occupies the summer months). In the last year they were collectively responsible for throwing 305,856 sticks with a doll-strike ratio of about 1 throw in 3.

Ba Game

Ba is a Scottish variant of medieval football, with added brutality. It is exciting, traditional, borderline barbaric in places, and several Scotsmen are hurt in the making. However, Scotland should be rightly proud of the Ba Game: a genuinely historic tradition that players and organisers have ensured has reached the twenty-first century in fine health.

The Ba Game resurrects ancient medieval football – more reminiscent of a Civil War re-enactment society than soccer – and traditionally occurs annually in the Orkneys. Kirkwall divides itself into Uppies (Up The Gates) and Doonies (Down The Gates), ensuring the next few hours are spent in unarmed combat while attempting to get a ball into the opposition's goal. How they do this is not seemingly controlled by anything as troublesome and invasive as rules. When Kirkwall Cathedral's bell strikes 1 p.m., the ball (manufactured from leather and recently donated by a German footwear company) is thrown into play, greeted by a cacophonous roar. The Doonies' goal is the sea – the sea presenting a fairly wide area to defend (there being 7,750 miles of British coastline) ought to give the Uppies an advantage. Indeed, the Uppies only required 2 hours 20 minutes to 'hail' (goal) the ball on Christmas Day 2010 and won again seven days later (the game is played on both Christmas and New Year's Day), a victory they repeated on New Year's Day 2012.

Another Orkney town, Stromness, also participates. In 1787, an island resident was moved to observe, 'football is the principal diversion of the common people.' Attempts have been made to ban the game in most centuries, including the twenty-first; an Orkney Islands Councillor informed the BBC during an unsuccessful attempt to dilute, if not outright ban, the

sport, 'Ba is a very physical sport and people do get hurt. There have been numerous people with broken bones and black eyes – and I saw a whole wall knocked down one year.' Currently the council underwrites the annual repair bill caused by the game, yet many locals remain incurably enthralled.

Ba is certainly a game for those not averse to disappointing their probation officer. On this day scary, wide-necked muscular toughness can return to the freedom of life without rule or law, and gets to shove people through shop windows with no troubling schedule adjustments for court appearances. That said, players are sensitive to injured colleagues, and play will cease to allow medical attention (though the injury had better be serious).

The ball is released simultaneous to the temporary suspension of restraining law. Adrenalin floods participants' bodies as players engage with immense commitment, showing real stomach for the fight, and displaying the appetite of men who have just discovered some barbecued chops after three months on the salad. A defiant refusal to acknowledge impending injury is heroically commonplace – though that's probably just the booze.

Players possess a perplexing willingness to stick the only head they'll ever have into a ruck of 200 energetic, maniacally borderline ruffians collectively fighting for the ball. Like other mass medieval football games, spectators must find themselves wondering how participants recognise which team other players represent, since they are devoid of kit distinctions, just the cluttered colours of 300 brawny brave islanders. Marshals are positioned intermittently around the contest, though there's an unpersuasive reassurance provided by their limited presence, as they look for potentially injurious scrimmaging. The noise is huge, and it would be hard for anyone to interject with an authoritative air over the top of the screaming, shouting, baying and, inevitably, the scrambled air ambulance.

In spite of warnings to the elderly, infirm and parked cars to avoid the area whenever the Ba Game is conducted, spectators line the route offering encouragement – and discouragement if they suspect the wrong team are in possession – with an unsettling verbosity and in the meantime the Marshals nobly struggle to police the boundary between hard-headed rationality and innate death wish.

Players deemed to have made a significant contribution to the Ba Game are carried aloft on team-mates' shoulders, and afterwards most players can be spotted in the pubs drinking like they're washing away the taste of defeat – or any functioning memory of success.

Bar Billiards
WORLD CHAMPIONSHIP

ow this is more like it. The Bar Billiards World Championship has been held in Jersey every year since inauguration in 1981, and the first thirty years has seen a ceaseless, uninterrupted chain of British world champions: the utter evisceration of the rest of the world awaits all non-British challengers. Had the Olympic organisation committee not outrageously rejected the sport, as a nation we could have made considerable progress decreasing our national deficit by stuffing numerous gold medals into envelopes addressed to 'Cash4Gold'. Well, the Olympics allow Beach Volleyball. And should you consider Beach Volleyball to be a more naturally telegenic sport, then be aware that Yorkshire TV regularly televised Bar Billiards throughout the 1970s. From a pub. In children's hour! Alongside darts and arm wrestling, *Indoor League* featured Bar Billiards recurrently accompanied by a commentator who would attempt to create

artificial excitement by declaring 'AND THE BAR IS DOWN!' in broadcasting tones usually reserved for first-hand witnessing of horrific world events like the Hindenburg explosion. (After about 15 minutes, balls are blocked from re-entering the game by a descending bar, signalling the game's imminent cessation.) Each episode would end with former cricketer and professional Yorkshireman Fred Trueman reclining in a pub chair, smoking a pipe and raising a pint of frothy ale to the viewer with the toast, 'Ah'll sithee.' Once again, worth pointing out . . . during children's TV! Oddly the game is now more common in the South than the North.

Given Bar Billiards is seen as a uniquely British sport, it may be surprising to discover that, like other perceived British institutions, its DNA reveals European origins, having almost certainly evolved from Russian Billiards – which, confusingly, is a Belgian not a Russian sport. Billiards Russe, as the French-speaking Belgians named it, was exported to the UK in the 1930s.

The game involves eight white balls augmented with one red. Potting a red ball provides double points – which tends to delay the game as players await the rolling return of the red ball after a pot, prior to continuing their break.

No, Bar Billiards probably doesn't provide fizzing electrical excitement among a super-charged captivated audience – but unlike billiards/pool/snooker which requires access to all four sides of the table, Bar Billiards players are limited to playing from just one table end – thus requiring only limited floor space, i.e. its main attribute being easier to ignore in a pub than pool. Eccentrically, it's only an enjoyable game to play if remaining below a certain line of competency; accomplished players can greedily consume the entire 15 minutes in one uninterrupted break, denying their opponent even a single visit to the table.

A Bar Billiards table is dissimilar to a conventional billiards/pool/snooker table due to one instantly noticeable modification: there are no pockets. Instead, nine holes appear in the table's surface. Players earn points by potting into the holes, with different values (ranging from 10 to 200 points) assigned to each. However, the large points-earners (100 and 200) are guarded by two white mushrooms and one black mushroom. Sounds odd, doesn't it? That's why they tend to call them pegs nowadays, but mushrooms were more fun. Knock over a white mushroom and your break is nullified; topple over the black peg and a player's entire match score is negated. Harsh.

The decline of the sport's natural habitat – the pub – has rapidly damaged the game's health (a county league secretary informed me that 84 pubs participated when he assumed duties in 1979 – now there are only 14 competing venues left). The tables, many of which are antiques, have found a collectors' market in the US. Yet Bar Billiards is a hugely important sport, inspiring us to become a nation of lobbyists to demand Olympic recognition. Why? 32 world championships held: 32 British world champions. That's why.

Black Pudding Throwing

W O R L D   C H A M P I O N S H I P

The Black Pudding Throwing Championship takes place in . . . well, go on, have a guess which half of the country stages this sport? Correct. It occurs annually in the North. Whereas Northerners can be 'earthy no-nonsense types' (or just 'rude' if you're not from the North), true Northerners justifiably insist to their Southern counterparts that the upper half of this Other Eden isn't a lazy stereotypical cliché involving whippets, black puddings and cloth caps – although, to be intrinsically fair, the latter two categories are decidedly easy to spot at this event. One competitor arrived wearing a huge over-sized cloth cap, which I initially assumed was a comment, both sartorial and satirical, on Southern perceptions of the North, though when I spotted several other similarly adorned participants, I concluded it could just be evergreen Northern fashion. In reality, they were channelling Ecky Thump from the *Goodies*.

Raised 30ft above the Lancashire market town of Ramsbottom, a dozen Yorkshire puddings sit on the wrong side of the Pennine border atop a high scaffold. The puddings stand precariously on a plinth, and it is up to the contestants to remove them by throwing three (real, not synthetic) black puddings. Puddings means points, and each contestant's score is measured by how many Yorkshire puddings they can dislodge. Throwers receive three throws (or 'chucks' in this part of the world), just like in darts, only with black puddings instead of darts. Obviously. Nothing weird about that. Rules state that only underarm throwing is permissible, and junior entrants aim at puddings positioned on a 20ft high plinth, with 10 concessionary feet removed.

Dislodged puddings in the adult contest are rare, owing to a combination of small targets raised 30ft in the air with the troublesome dexterity encountered when projecting a black pudding. Results show it's an unsurprisingly low-scoring affair – so low-scoring it transpires, with puddings proving difficult to raze (to the ground), that draws are common. Even the final has previously been decided by a 'pudding-off'.

The event's administrators unsuccessfully lobbied and lobbed for London 2012 Olympic inclusion, even producing the sport's own logo in anticipation of acceptance: five circular puddings representational of the Olympic rings.

During the 2010 Black Pudding World Throwing Championship, one contestant received a relatively serious shoulder injury – not sustained during the hurling itself, but celebrating a successful throw by dancing rather exuberantly in a skip; he was named as Mad John.

Attracting high-flying athletes and black puddings from all around the globe (well, mainly the central Lancashire area), organisers ensured Black Pudding Hurling was the unofficial demonstration sport of the Commonwealth Games when the event came to rainy Manchester in 2002.

Bognor Birdman

They say that the footsteps of a condemned man emit no sound – though that could just be because they've had death row carpeted. The performers huddled backstage (or rather, backpier) for this sport can be just as quiet – they're about to jump several metres off a pier with only a pair of papier-mâché wings enabling them to defy all known laws of physics. When it comes to defying laws, physics is a pretty big one to pick a fight with – maybe a minor council byelaw would have been easier.

This is hardcore eccentric – jumping off a 40ft pier in fancy dress while attempting to fly a home-made aeroplane (there are some nouns that 'home-made'

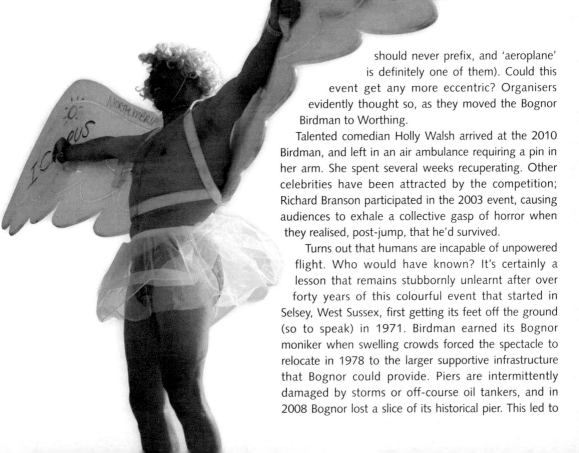

should never prefix, and 'aeroplane' is definitely one of them). Could this event get any more eccentric? Organisers evidently thought so, as they moved the Bognor Birdman to Worthing.

Talented comedian Holly Walsh arrived at the 2010 Birdman, and left in an air ambulance requiring a pin in her arm. She spent several weeks recuperating. Other celebrities have been attracted by the competition; Richard Branson participated in the 2003 event, causing audiences to exhale a collective gasp of horror when they realised, post-jump, that he'd survived.

Turns out that humans are incapable of unpowered flight. Who would have known? It's certainly a lesson that remains stubbornly unlearnt after over forty years of this colourful event that started in Selsey, West Sussex, first getting its feet off the ground (so to speak) in 1971. Birdman earned its Bognor moniker when swelling crowds forced the spectacle to relocate in 1978 to the larger supportive infrastructure that Bognor could provide. Piers are intermittently damaged by storms or off-course oil tankers, and in 2008 Bognor lost a slice of its historical pier. This led to

pier-pressure (really couldn't resist) to move the event to neighbouring Worthing, but in 2010 it returned to Bognor. Unfortunately, Worthing wouldn't unfurl its clasped grip on Bognor Birdman, and so two staggered events were staged in both Worthing and Bognor in 2010; it's also routinely known as International Birdman, which takes the pressure off the whole is-it-a-Bognor-or-Worthing prefix?

Different categories of participation are allocated by organisers (termed Condor and Kingfisher), ranging from hang-gliders to everyone's favourites: valiant eccentrics in colourful costumes piloting makeshift contraptions. Holly Walsh (above), with co-pilot

former World Gravy Wrestling Champion Joel Hicks, flew a home-made helicopter.

Tantalisingly near to the 100-metre mark, Steve Elkins succeeded in flying 99.8 metres in 2009, comfortably accomplishing the furthest distance yet flown in the competition's history. The fact that an eye-popping £30,000 prize (supplementing the main prize of £550) would have been awarded for reaching the 100-metre mark ensured inevitable controversy; the prize has subsequently been quietly downgraded to a still-worth-bagging £10k. Yet the organisers deploy high-tech equipment to measure flying distance, using 'three electronic theodolites'. A cash prize is also awarded to the participant who stays airborne the longest, regardless of distance covered.

Birdman is a wonderfully good-humoured event celebrating outermost British eccentricity and creative home-made costume design, raising money for good causes and providing a tremendous day out for everyone (well, apart from poor Holly – though she forged the superb Edinburgh show *Hollycopter* from the experience, demonstrating with a Venn diagram how Birdman is fancy dress coupled with suicide bids). Cancellation of both 2011 Birdmans (Bognor and Worthing) due to high winds prompted Holly to remark, 'if this had happened last year, I wouldn't have a broken elbow or an Edinburgh show.'

Britain is undoubtedly richer for Birdman's existence. Long may it soar.

Bottle-Kicking

There's no kicking involved, and bottles don't feature at any stage – but other than that, the sport is self-explanatory. It's certainly an early indication of the general level of logical reasoning involved in a terrifyingly dangerous eccentric sport, with two teams of seemingly random personnel simultaneously harbouring a baffling desire to carry a small keg from one hedge to another. For reasons never clearly established, 300 people representing two almost identical parts of Leicestershire challenge, barge and generally hospitalise each other in a quest for tossing a miniature wooden keg over a minor stream. It's a rather non-descript stream, not a babbling brook worthy of inspiring Tennyson to purposefully open his notebook.

Both the origins – and presumably the point – of the game have gone missing in history. There are competing accounts of the game's beginnings,

and perhaps the most intriguing theory advanced for the custom's foundation recounts how two women were taking an ill-advised short-cut through a field, when they received unwelcomed bovine attention. The situation rapidly deteriorated when a bull began to chase them. As a garrotting looked the likeliest end to an otherwise pleasant country walk, a hare came to the rescue and saw off the marauding bull (nothing odd about that story). Symbolising their gratitude to God, the two ladies donated money for the 'miracle' to be remembered by the poor of the Leicestershire village of Hallaton receiving a feast.

Although donating money for the village to receive a 'Beware of the Bull' sign might have been more practical, instead they decreed that each Easter the vicar would provide loaves, beer and – here's the insensitive bit – a hare pie. Well, that's gratitude for you: a HARE pie! Oh well, hare today . . .

Proving there was such a thing as a free lunch led to unforeseen skirmishes, as local beneficiaries rejected patient queueing, preferring to aggressively grab at the gratis grub and beverages that had been bequeathed to them each year. This was begrudgingly tolerated by the clergy (although a vicar who attempted to ban the riotous feast in 1790 awoke to 'No pie, no parson' daubed on his vicarage wall), until one Easter Monday a delegation from the neighbouring village of Medbourne arrived, demonstrating a premeditated objective to steal the beer and return it to their village.

Hence an inter-village battle was created, explaining today's custom of Bottle-Kicking being prefixed by hare pie spread over the fields (it's supposedly inedible – so the two ladies' choice of gift was clearly poorly researched). Following a church service, fragments of the pie are tossed between combatants, like a messier non-vegetarian variation of the All Blacks' Haka – prior to battle commencing between Hallaton and the tarnished beer-stealers of Medbourne.

Yes, the winning side does get to share a small barrel of beer (permitting a sip each at best), but after being pointlessly hurled around the Leicestershire countryside all afternoon, it is unsurprisingly shaken to such a violent extent that pulling out the stopper is akin to activating a hand grenade.

Just in case the sport was considered too namby-pamby-girly-wirly soft, several barbed-wire fences are left in the playing area, augmented by many dangerous holes. One player gets snagged on the barbed wire, and becomes a makeshift bridge as other participants use him as a prostrate plank to see-saw themselves over the razor wire. Finally one team reaches the 'goal' – or, more accurately, dyke, and then lobs the miniature barrel over the stream to a recipient on the other side. Anyone hoping they can now escape this madness only has a short-lived euphoria to enjoy, as it's immediately apparent that the whole spectacle must recommence and the pastoral idyll will be destroyed for another couple of hours. Players conduct quick checks by counting to two in order to confirm they still possess the regulatory prescribed two eyes, ears, legs and arms; looking worried, tired, bruised and hopelessly aware there's still no ambulance access to these fields.

A different painted wooden keg is used for each game, until the next year when any survivors reconvene on Easter Monday in the same field. A former organiser and event doyen informed the BBC, 'The rules are very simple: there aren't any. There are a few injuries, such as broken bones and things like that but most people are unharmed and the emergency services are on standby throughout.' Had the BBC sent a more thorough investigative journalist, he may have asked about the hastily dug shallow graves that had recently appeared across the field.

Tips and advice for participants: Don't. It's utterly insane. Nevertheless, it is a magnificent occasion to witness, preserving and celebrating a truly unique British sporting heritage.

Brambles Cricket

Cricket. The sound of leather on willow, a cut to the rhododendrons, church tower shadow creeping over the village green as play approaches stumps, the foghorn of a passing oil tanker, the low roar of a lifeboat's engine come to rescue the slip cordon. Eh?

No matter how wet the English summer gets, this is the wettest cricket match in existence. And that's because this cricket match takes place in the middle of the English Channel. I'll type that again: this cricket match takes place in the English Channel. No, not floating on it. In. The. Sea.

For one hour a year, the gravitational pull of the mid-August moon is sufficiently powerful to ensure the tide parts to reveal a sandbank in the Solent. The protruding sandbank can be hazardous – *Queen Elizabeth II* got stranded here in 2008 (the cruise liner, not the ageing monarch).

Members of Cowes Sailing Club challenge Hamble's Royal Southern Yacht Club to an annual game. Knee-deep in seawater puddles, you wonder what happens if it rains? Perhaps they would go off for a light shower? Ducks are common, but thankfully drownings are not – as long as they ensure they leave as soon as the clock signifies one hour has elapsed, as the waters soon close above the sandbank, hiding it for another 364 days and 23 hours.

Isle of Wight boat builder Uffa Fox is credited with starting the game – possibly in the early 1960s (no one's quite sure when – which is odd, 'cos if I'd started a cricket match in the middle of the sea, it may be something I would remember). Initially, the annual game was Fox's XI challenging a side from the Holmwood Hotel in Cowes.

After Fox's death, this aquatic cricketing tradition was in danger of dissipating, until another local boat builder, Tom Richardson, provided the kiss of life to the game (and probably several players unwisely fielding in the deep). Also known for acting in TV's eighties blockbuster series *Howards' Way*, Richardson has captained both ocean-going vessels and ocean-going cricket teams. The game has been contested each year without interruption (come high tide or high water) since 1984, with the two rival boating clubs continuing the watery cricket tradition. Rather charmingly, each team takes it in turns to win.

Alcohol is often an inseparable part of both cricket and yachting, so drinks are readily served and bottles swigged during the game, ensuring one part of the sandbank is definitely not dry. A Pimms bar is opened to entertain spectators for the gaps in play caused by the stumps floating away in the wash whenever a cruise-liner passes, which appears to be a perennial problem.

British Open Crabbing
CHAMPIONSHIP

If there's one pastime Britain's guaranteed to dominate, it's going on holiday to a seaside resort and catching crabs. The Open was started in 1981 by the town's youth club to raise funds for the local Blythburgh hospital. The action occurs in a delightfully, almost Wodehousian, village mellifluously named Walberswick (near Southwold in Suffolk). Entries have been ascending each year, with 762 in 2007, 978 in 2008, 1,252 in 2009, escalating to such an extent that organisers reluctantly rested the Open in 2011 to conduct research into the event's future sustainability.

Many children participate, although the event enforces an official entrance age limit: 'no one born before 1890 can participate' – which sounds harsh, but to be fair I only witnessed 2 or 3 severely disappointed old people dejectedly shuffling back to their cars.

After every available space – and some unavailable spaces, when a bit of light pushing occurs just before the start time – is occupied both in and out of the shallow water, a signal notifies contestants that they have 90 minutes to catch as many crabs as they can. Bait is an essential stopping off point on any crab's

journey between open sea and keep net, so pre-fishing conversation is dominated by the subject. One child is clearly using cheeseburger fragments on his line, while others go for the even less edible. Indeed, smelly seems to be the only common orthodoxy among bait choices. One parent counsels their offspring against using a Twix.

Eventually the largest catches are weighed (winners are declared by accrued catch weight, not number of crabs caught) and winners announced. Margins separating victory from defeat can be minuscule, so reweighing regularly occurs. The winner receives an engraved silver plate, a cheque for £50 and several small jars of crab paste – which the winner has to be reminded to take when he attempts to leave without the paste.

Overall, the event predominantly exists to raise money for charity and is one of the most age inclusive events I've ever witnessed – though I would strongly advise any crabs to avoid the area during the first Sunday in August.

Bumps Races

ere indisputably posh Cuthbert Lempriere Holthouse holds a semi-reluctant pose, captured in 1910 with the last ever wooden spoon awarded by Cambridge University. If you think his spoon is impractically big, you should see his accompanying cup of tea just out of shot.

The first thing you need to know about Eights Week, or Bumps Races, is that the number of people who crew an eight during Eights Week is . . . (go on, have a guess) . . . nine. The second thing you need to know about Eights Week is that Eights Week lasts for, as the name implies, er, ahem, four days. And these are Oxford and Cambridge University intelligentsia!

Because the River Isis (or Thames to you and me) and River Cam are both inconveniently narrow for staging boat racing, teams comprising different Oxford and Cambridge colleges row in procession, charged with the objective to pursue the boat ahead. Thus they set off at equally spaced intervals. Once the stern of the boat ahead has been reached then crossed, they are deemed to have 'bumped it', rendering them now eligible to swap places in the next day's starting grid. The level of focussed seriousness is ludicrous, as is the muscular oarsmen to boathouse groupies ratio. However, a common recurring accusation is nearly always invalid: namely the fielding of ringers. A few years ago Magdalen College allegedly packed their side with members of the German Olympic rowing team. 'Foul!' cried other colleges (not as Magdalen's boat was ever going to be within earshot as they were already so far up the Thames they'd probably reached Lechlade).

Yet rowers genuinely attend colleges – and not in a token turn-up-for-a-photo-shoot and one lecture way. Ratcheting up the eccentricity, winning boats are traditionally burned like a Viking's funeral.

Oxford pulverised favourites Cambridge in the 2011 Boat Race, getting so far in front that they could choose their own line (the Boat Race is unique in distance, and rowing rarely includes corners), and all Varsity Boat Race competitors learn their craft in the annual Bumps Races. To be a successful rower at this level requires three attributes: dedication, natural strength and a reliable alarm clock – as training is conducted in the 6 a.m. to 8 a.m. slot.

Attending training sessions for Bumps Races reveals lots of small shouty people with Napoleon complexes getting in the way of recreational towpath users, bellowing mystifying instructions at insouciant training eights.

Races commence when a loud starting gun is fired. Moreover, on closer inspection it isn't just a starting gun – that would be too utilitarian for Oxford and Cambridge; they actually use a real cannon!

Crews race in several different divisions over the four days, racing in thirteen boats per heat. Where they finish this year determines their starting order for next year's event. Colleges are inexplicably proud of their 'bumps', and students regularly adorn college quad walls with crudely chalked pictures of their conquests resembling prehistoric cave paintings. The lower division teams start earliest in the day, alternating between men's and women's races, culminating in the first division races which conclude each day. The hindmost division teams reward the casual spectator with eccentric behaviour; some teams undermine the event with Swiftonian satire, appearing in fancy dress, consuming a wicker-basket picnic, and trailing a lazy hand in the water. It's an enjoyable contrast to the high division races, where coxes can genuinely be heard shouting out rousing motivational lines. The climax of 2011's Bumps Races ended with one crew 'catching a crab' when contesting the lead – no, not an inappropriately timed spot of fishing, but rowing jargon referring to an unreleased oar acting as a brake.

College rowing was taken extremely seriously in the nineteenth century, and dedication to the college boat was responsible for many fourth class degrees. The tradition of wooden spoons is linked to Oxford and Cambridge Bumps Races, as original wooden spoons were impractically large affairs, often made from college oars – though awarded to the lowest degree in that academic year, rather than the captain of the slowest boat.

Cheese Rolling

ow officially banned, though others more optimistically reappraise the event's death as merely hibernation, Cheese Rolling takes place on a Gloucestershire hillside at Cooper's Hill (rumours of unofficial comebacks have proved prophetic, when enthusiasts succeeded in staging a similar event in the locale in May 2011). While most participants, spectators and reporters routinely refer to the area as a hillside, someone benefiting from superior topographical expertise may be able to point out the difference between a hillside and A Sheer Drop. Physical geography semantics aside, this is a terrifying gradient. A ratio of 1:3 becoming 1:2 I'd say (and that's the ratio of participants to St John Ambulance volunteers).

This sport is eccentricity to the max – weapons grade eccentricity. I asked a contestant in the last permitted Cheese Roll (no, not a reference to the buffet closing) what would prompt him to return to competitive cheese-chasing.

'Nothing,' he answers with surprising rationality.

'£1 million?'

'No, 'cos I wouldn't win it.'

Cheese Rolling is mad. Madder than a psychopathic madman with a stubbed toe dressed as the Mad Hatter. And you certainly need to be mad to participate in it; I'm tempted to say 'crackers', but I won't. Yet it remains undisputedly one of the maddest events it is possible – or more accurately, was possible – to compete in for the off-chance of winning cheese, given that so much of contemporary British life has been sprayed with the fun-killing disinfectant of Health and Safety. Genuflecting towards the twin false gods of Health and Safety is one thing, but not everything atrophied by the H&S Exec is without justification. And you can, kind of, see their point here.

Contestants – and several hundred are attracted each May Bank Holiday – run (or, more accurately, fall) downhill in blinkered pursuit of a 7lb cheese. The winner (i.e. the person who reaches the cheese at the bottom of the hill ahead of the rest of the field without being pronounced medically dead at the scene) keeps

the wheel of Double Gloucester cheese – although it may well have been Single Gloucester, but everyone was now seeing double.

Ludicrously steep in places, it resembles a cliff rather than a hill. Cheese may cause dreams, but this induces nightmares. Some participants strap on bandaged joint supports, an act of futile optimism akin to Japanese kamikaze pilots wearing goggles.

When the charge commences, there is a collective cry that resonates across the hillside like an ancient battlefield. A tumultuous din erupts, terrified bird flocks ascend from trees, yet there is also a far uglier sound – just thinking of the noise again means I'm putting my hands over my ears years later: it's the snap of something serious, like a bone or tendon, or more likely both. Previous winners have referred to experiencing such sounds, but a combination of bravery, off-the-scale stupidity and gravity kept them going towards the finishing line in focused cheese pursuit. It's hard cheese if you win, hard cheese if you don't.

Chess Boxing

Any event that would result in a prolonged custodial sentence if it took place outside the venue, shouldn't qualify as a sport. Perhaps primitive pugnacious pugilism has never really appealed to me but getting repeatedly whacked in the face seems an odd choice of leisure activity.

Chess, however, I do like – although there's rarely a satisfactory conclusion to games once a certain level of competency has been reached. For example, most senior level games conclude with offered resignation many moves before checkmate. Chess must be the only sport where players can never be bothered to finish a game, therefore, clearly, it requires more action, violence and excitement, while boxing requires less physicality and more cerebral focusing. Thus the hybrid Chess Boxing was created.

The game's appeal lies within its contradictions – soldering physical hardness onto mental agility, a marriage of brains and brawn without anyone being saddled with the ugly one. Although the game is Dutch in origin, Britain has emerged as a world leader in the sport, embracing it more consistently than almost all other nations. That means we're big. And clever. Other commentators remain unconvinced, including an ITV reporter who branded the sport 'part physical, part intellectual, entirely mental'; it's rather difficult to argue with that.

Matches commence with four minutes of chess followed by a two-minute boxing round (though some contests decree three minutes). Competitors then receive a one-minute break (presumably spent unhygienically spitting water marbled with blood over a chess board, while a shadowy coach figure who probably once drank with the Krays appears in the corner, draping a towel over his boxer's shoulders, and whispers in his ear, 'He's vulnerable to a queen's bishop gambit counteracting his over-reliance on the King's Indian Defence'). Meanwhile a mini-skirted blonde double-tasks by holding aloft a board proclaiming 'Round Two' while simultaneously pouting in a manner relatively unseen since the era of 1950s movie starlets.

Rules were quickly changed once the sport became more formalised, and chess boxers now routinely wear headphones while playing, counteracting any tactical advice offered by supporters. Headphones are not required for the boxing portion, given that pugilistic advice tends to discourage tactically aware sophisticates – 'Hit 'im! Hit 'im! Hit 'im!' being the more insightful shared advice; participants are unlikely to interpret this as revelatory counsel.

To have an arm raised aloft by the referee, winners must either checkmate or knock out their opponent; should neither half of this sporting hybrid provide a winner, then a victor is announced on boxing points. Should scores still be inseparable, then it is declared a draw.

All the action occurs within a traditional boxing ring. Although moderate boxing abilities can be sufficient to win a contest, inadequate chess abilities would be exposed quickly, as speed chess rules apply (i.e. players only have a few minutes in which to complete the game).

There is nearly always a visible result outcome – and this does provide Chess Boxing with an advantage over the traditional board game. Conventional chess doesn't exactly treat audiences to a spectacle. Even in a game where neither player has gained a material advantage – with pieces and pawns inseparably level – one player will suddenly push over his king in a moody flick of resignation. Most pundits present then nod verbal agreement with this decision, extrapolating the strategic inevitability leading to unavoidable defeat for black that would occur in the next 14 moves. Perhaps this could be imported into football, where after a goalless opening 35 minutes, Chelsea could mystifyingly resign and concede defeat to Arsenal for enjoying an undisputable territorial advantage. Alan Hansen and Gary Lineker could then explain why this would lead to an inevitable Arsenal victory, and the crowd could all get a much earlier train.

Clog Cobbing

For several centuries the humble clog was the protective footwear of choice for the nation's workers clattering across factory floors. Of course, Britain proudly has form when it comes to throwing around footwear in the industrial workplace; the Luddites opted to hurl their clogs into the newly automated machinery – something they must have regretted during the barefooted walk home. By the twentieth century, better and less crude workplace footwear had become affordable, so the clog fell into disuse. By the early twenty-first century, factories fell into disuse too and everyone worked at call centres or 'did something in IT'. Hence Clog Cobbing celebrates the anachronistic industrial footwear. In a hundred years time someone will probably inaugurate a Throwing the Teleworker Headset World Championship.

Lancashire looks good in the sun – sunshine suits it; in fact, it should definitely wear it more often. Sunshine greeted the start of 2011's event, held each Easter Monday at the side of the Roebuck Inn in Rossendale, Lancashire.

Hurling a factory clog backwards high into the Lancastrian afternoon, as participants are required to do by the rules, offers no visibility to the thrower as to where his discarded shoe will be aimed or, critically, land. Thus projectile direction is as unpredictable as a grapefruit squirt. Throwing blind and backwards – contestants must stand with their back to the throwing-line – ensures acute randomness, which in turn ensures a random distribution of prizes.

There is an irremovable obstacle to avoid at this event: the town's river looms large like a huge gaping bunker on a small golf green, seemingly sucking in players' otherwise glory-bound clogs. After only a few minutes it becomes undeniably obvious that the competition is being staged too close to the river, surely leaving officials to conclude that a necessary change should be made. And yet they refuse, citing that it would be 'impractical' to alter the course of the river.

Competitors have three throws, but must grip the clog by either the heel, toe or tongue prior to despatching it through the (usually moist) Lancastrian air. The event record stands at a genuinely impressive 30 metres.

Coal Carrying
W O R L D   C H A M P I O N S H I P

Coal's future has been chartered as one in irreversible decline, redolent of a global tilt away from fossil fuels towards sustainable energy – but the World Coal Carrying Championships are expanding annually in popularity, and may survive beyond the last pit, akin to the greater longevity of colliery bands than the pits where they were founded. Future spectators at this event may well be overheard asking, 'Mummy, what's coal?' as competitors strain to carry solar heating panels towards the uphill finishing line.

Yet there's one irrefutable future truth: the competitors who enter this event will always be seriously fit, with the men's event requiring participants to carry a 50kg bag (that's practically 8 stone in old money) for a distance just shy of a mile. It's difficult to find any sport, professional or amateur, requiring such a physical commitment. By comparison, the ladies are shown a partial kindness in being requested to merely lug 25kg of coal over a mile – very much the definition of a relative kindness.

START
GAWTHORPE WORLD
COAL CARRYING
CHAMPIONSHIPS
EVERY
EASTER MONDAY
SPONSORED BY

BOX

Eric F. Box (Funeral Directors) Ltd.
EMAIL funerals@efbox.co.uk
Telephone:

43

The event has been staged for forty-eight consecutive years, with three professions repeatedly proving to be the required day job for being a world champion coal carrier: farmer, builder and window cleaner; oddly, coal deliveryman fails to make the list.

Local testimony consistently dates the sport's origins to 1963, tracing its genesis to the traditional birthing pool responsible for many eccentric British sports entering the world: two inebriated blokes arguing in a pub. Specifically, a pub in the West Yorkshire village of Gawthorpe, and an argument overseen by the chairman of the village's May Pole committee – an origin nicely acknowledged by the finishing requirement that coal sacks must be placed at the foot of the village May Pole to signify the end of the race. Given the grimacing resolve required to carry coal for a mile – the course includes a sadistically steep ascent prior to carriers doubling back on themselves – the event is noticeably lacking in frivolity and fancy dress, with serious athletes focusing on winning the prize money to spend on chiropractors.

Holding six of the fastest finishing times in the race's history is world record holder David Jones of Meltham, West Yorkshire; he completed the course in an astounding 4 minutes 6 seconds in 1991, and repeated the same accomplishment in 1995 when he matched his own world record. And just think of the fuss they made over Roger Bannister taking just 6 seconds less to compete a slightly longer distance

with the black and white footage clearly showing Bannister was NOT hauling a bag of coal – what a soft Southerner! Ruth Clegg claimed the women's world record in 2008, when completing a hat-trick of world champion titles, carrying her 25kg bag in a mere 5 minutes and 3 seconds – impressive until realising that most women's handbags usually weigh around 25kg.

Tips for participation: don't. It's completely insane. And you wouldn't be fit enough, anyway. Oh, and don't paint broken lumps of polystyrene black, as you can't bring your own coal sack.

Conkers

WORLD CHAMPIONSHIP

hen I was fourteen, desperate for fifteen, an older cohort recounted a mesmeric tale to fellow schoolboys, describing how he'd lost his virginity under a chestnut tree. Being young, I just considered this careless, and questioned whether he'd looked hard enough for it (he assured me he had). Epilogue: The girl proclaimed as being my older schoolfriend's sexual conquest denied the story, and called him a 'pathetic, small-knobbed liar' in front of the youth club

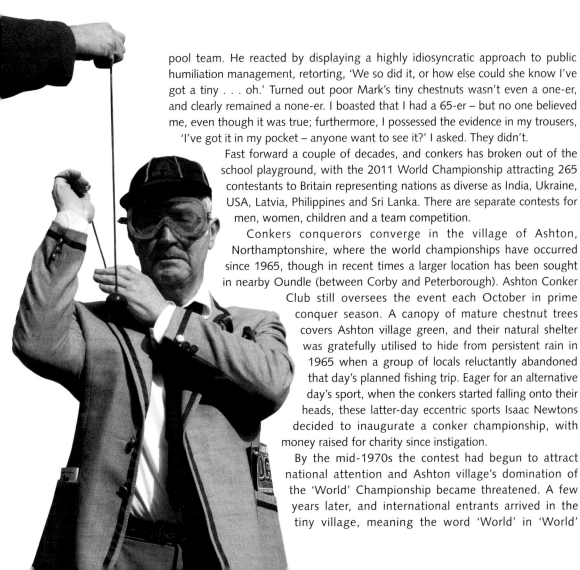

pool team. He reacted by displaying a highly idiosyncratic approach to public humiliation management, retorting, 'We so did it, or how else could she know I've got a tiny . . . oh.' Turned out poor Mark's tiny chestnuts wasn't even a one-er, and clearly remained a none-er. I boasted that I had a 65-er – but no one believed me, even though it was true; furthermore, I possessed the evidence in my trousers, 'I've got it in my pocket – anyone want to see it?' I asked. They didn't.

Fast forward a couple of decades, and conkers has broken out of the school playground, with the 2011 World Championship attracting 265 contestants to Britain representing nations as diverse as India, Ukraine, USA, Latvia, Philippines and Sri Lanka. There are separate contests for men, women, children and a team competition.

Conkers conquerors converge in the village of Ashton, Northamptonshire, where the world championships have occurred since 1965, though in recent times a larger location has been sought in nearby Oundle (between Corby and Peterborough). Ashton Conker Club still oversees the event each October in prime conquer season. A canopy of mature chestnut trees covers Ashton village green, and their natural shelter was gratefully utilised to hide from persistent rain in 1965 when a group of locals reluctantly abandoned that day's planned fishing trip. Eager for an alternative day's sport, when the conkers started falling onto their heads, these latter-day eccentric sports Isaac Newtons decided to inaugurate a conker championship, with money raised for charity since instigation.

By the mid-1970s the contest had begun to attract national attention and Ashton village's domination of the 'World' Championship became threatened. A few years later, and international entrants arrived in the tiny village, meaning the word 'World' in 'World'

Championship legitimately lost its inverted commas when the trophy was Mexico-bound in 1976. However, this was not necessarily progress as in 1998 a German won the championship – albeit not on penalties for once. As Americans repeatedly prove with baseball, there is little point in staging a world championship in a quaintly parochial sport if it risks compromising the home nation's dominance. By all means allow Germany to be world champions in minor sports (football, tennis, motor racing), but not conkers!

Sometimes an outwardly even game will end in a spectacular explosion, with conker shrapnel distributed over a huge radius. However, strict rules ensure that each victor must commence their next game with a new conker, thus insensitively denying

players the opportunity to have a two-er, four-er, eight-er, etc.

Contests are well policed, as two stewards are allocated to each game, along with a Chief Umpire's door to knock on for decisions that cannot be satisfactorily rectified by stewards and players alone. One of their primary concerns governs the lace length, which the rules stipulate, 'must be no less than a distance of 8 inches between nut and knuckle.'

Games are prescribed to last for a maximum of 5 minutes; should nuts still be untarnished after 5 minutes of frantic swinging, then players are permitted three more triple strikes each. Should stalemate still ensue, then the player adjudged to have registered the highest total of direct hits will win the match. Even at supposedly the highest level of competitive conkers, a swing and a miss are not uncommon.

Should a player's nut (I'm going to refer to them as conkers – it avoids ambiguity and sniggering at the back) become dislodged and bounce onto the floor, this does not mean the game is over. Instead, one of the stewards merely conducts a damage inspection, and if the conker is considered to be in a reasonably unbroken state – i.e. rises before the culmination of a steward's count to ten and the conker is capable of recognising the correct amount of fingers the other referee is holding aloft – then it can be rethreaded back onto its lace, and play will continue.

Crazy Golf

WORLD CHAMPIONSHIP

ark Twain perfectly described golf in a famous and oft-used quotation: 'golf is shit'. It's also a good walk spoiled. Golf's association with Rupert Bear trousers and damming the flow of social mobility tends to ensure several people mark it down on their score card, although the sport did bask in subsequent back page to front page attention thanks to Tiger Woods playing a round (in a different way to usual).

I'm at the Crazy Golf World Championship enduring an unnecessarily loud business guy brokering a deal on his mobile. His wife looks bored, his children look bored, his unborn baby probably looks bored too – they're all wearing a wearisome 'yeah, we know – we have to live with this twat' expression. He informs the unfortunate person on the other end of the phone, and the surrounding 200 people in our vicinity, that he's excited about a deal.

'I'm excited about this deal.' (Told you.) 'I've got a big feeling in my trousers about this one.' Two hundred strangers briefly share a commonality, a collective desire to see him being splattered to death with mini-golf clubs. However, thankfully, players' concentration levels are sufficiently high to block out ignorant mobile-phone man, based on the evidence of their putting which is remarkably impressive, as several spectators visibly wonder whether to have a whip-round to enable his suffering wife to abscond.

Only a small percentage of the population regularly crunch their way along the gravel drives that lead to Britain's often aggressively expensive golf clubs, whereas Crazy Golf ultimately democratises the game. And golf, so often perceived – albeit unfairly – as being a privately run dictatorship, is in immense need of democratising revolution.

The Crazy Golf World Championships commenced in Hastings in 2003, and has been endearingly known as 'nutters with putters' ever since. Players (or 'nutters' if you insist) complete six rounds (three each on two different courses), a process which sifts out the lowest scoring (remember, that's conceptually good in golf) eighteen players to compete in a final round to determine the winner. Welshman Tim 'Ace Man' Davies has somewhat dominated the event, winning the coveted title five times. His record average round score was 34 – not bad for 18 holes, given it took me 34 shots to complete one hole after some negligent individuals had absent-mindedly left a miniature windmill on the course.

With winners announced and participants securely back at the nineteenth hole (apparently that's how golf people refer to the club house), shouty mobile-phone man is outside smoking and returning to his

inevitable 4x4 TurboCruiserPlanetRuiner™. He's still on his mobile, and still shouting 'I've got a really big feeling in my head; I can really feel this one!' Surely that's someone's cue to whack him like a Par 5 tee shot over the head with a discarded putter. No one in Hastings would give evidence, other than to declare that the *Crazy Golf World Championship* is another great British achievement providing perpetual British world champions.

Cross-Channel Swimming Race

Responsible for more goose fat-smearing than a middle class dinner party's perfect roast potatoes, contestants traditionally dive into what has become known by its very own cliché as 'the M25 of shipping lanes'. Such is the volume of shipping traffic in the English Channel that avoiding it as a swimmer is rendered almost impossible. Hence crossing such a nautical motorway requires an accompanying crew and a suspended sense of fear. A head constantly bobbing above and below the water line like a Halloween apple in a barrel is not an ideal vantage point to scan for 360

degree dangers. Thus the support boat's crew have to constantly alter course, or even reverse to avoid being sucked towards ship's propellers – modern nautical radar not yet being accomplished at picking up grease-covered swimmers.

The *Daily Mail* inaugurated an international Cross-Channel Swimming Race in 1951. The early years were dominated by three countries: Britain (unsurprisingly), France (unsurprisingly) and Egypt (surprisingly). Indeed, the first winner was Egyptian Army Lieutenant Hassen Abdel Rehim – one of only nine to complete the swim out of the twenty-

four that had earlier bravely dived in at Dover. The participants competing for a generous £1,000 prize (remember this was 1951) contained eight females, and the women's title went to divinity teacher Eileen Fenton from Dewsbury, Yorkshire. Swimming the final stages in spite of only possessing one operational arm, she was greeted on the Calais rocks by an encounter with a typically foul-breathed amorous Frenchman – when a dog licked her face!

Billy Butlin, the holiday camp magnate, assumed sponsorship duties from 1953, and Egyptians continued to dominate the race, especially Rehim and his compatriot Mahri Hassan Hamad. When the 1956 Suez Crisis erupted, inflamed by somewhat asinine British governance, Butlin allegedly refused to accept Egyptian entrants in the race. British and French swimmers were reluctant to swim in what had now become polluted waters (I mean metaphorically, this

time), and consequently the event was discontinued for over 50 years, until its planned resurrection finally occurred in 2009.

Alison Streeter, known as the Queen of the English Channel, has completed a record 43 crossings; by now, you'd have thought she would have discovered there was a ferry. Bulgarian Petar Stoychev became the fastest ever channel crosser in 2007 when he touched the shore in France only 6 hours and 57 minutes after leaving Dover – an indisputably fast time in comparison to the very first cross-channel swimmer: proud Briton and Victorian Captain Matthew Webb; he probably gained added buoyancy from his *de rigueur* period moustache, when completing his historic breaststroke swim in 1875 in just under 22 hours. Unfortunately he died in 1883 while attempting to swim the notorious Whirlpool Rapids beneath Niagara Falls.

Custard Pie
WORLD CHAMPIONSHIP

levating the evergreen comedy standby of a custard pie in the face to the status of a sport may be over-egging it (both concept and pie). Yet skilled throwers deploy aerodynamic dexterity to achieve accuracy and points, a generous six points being available for a direct facial hit, and up to five for witty costumes and inventive throwing techniques. The competition must also double as the World's Worst Waiter/Waitress Championship. This is about as messy as it's possible to get in the sporting arena.

Attending several eccentric sports events in quick succession renders it moderately unsurprising to spot a tiger wandering around at this event – on two legs and reading the *Daily Mirror* – though he takes an early pie in the face and is eliminated in the first round, failing to claw back any momentum after his stripes become instantly obscured by pie stains. Several teams also compete in fancy dress, which must lead to a lot of arguments about deposits being waived on Monday morning at the fancy dress hire shop. Ironically, the 2010 winners were a team entered by a local cleaning company. Also entered were the politically insensitive team named the Kraut Girls – who turned out to be (a) actually from Germany and (b) men. The modern world can be a confusing place. However, the rest of

the world proved no match for Coxheath village, as local foursome Coxheath 'til I Pie were declared chief splatterers, knocking out semi-finalists Pie Noon en route to yellow glory.

Operating under the alias of 'Mr Pastry', the tournament's chef bakes bespoke pies for the event. Taste and quality ingredients are downgraded by the necessity to ensure the pies have the correct consistency for providing good aerodynamic ability, coupled with providing the satisfying audibility of a 'slap' sound, followed by a slow sticky roll-down once a victim has been hit – exactly the same culinary priorities that were deployed by an Indian restaurant I frequented as a student. Apparently the trick is to use lots of flour, water, yellow colouring and an unrevealed secret ingredient (which we're assuming is safe to eat).

Teams hurl five pies in the first heat, rising to ten in the final, with judges assiduously awarding three points for a shoulder hit, one point for body contact, while a direct facial hit is deemed a six-pointer. Two points are deducted for consecutive misses, though points can be randomly added for amusing throwing techniques, fancy dress and comic improvisation – there's not a sport in existence that couldn't be immeasurably improved by this rule.

By the time the winners are announced, the audience will have witnessed more competitive tarts and aimless flinging of frothy stuff at each other than an episode of *Loose Women*.

Contesting the 44th annual pie fight in 2011, teams had travelled from around Europe. Event originator Mike Fitzgerald conceived the inaugural pie fight in June 1967 to raise funds for a village hall in Coxheath – located a few miles from Maidstone, Kent – where he later became mayor. Present at nearly all subsequent annual events, he informed the BBC, 'A lot of people come from office jobs and are pleased to get outside. You get bankers and people who work in building societies and they just like to let go. They dress up for it as well so people don't know who they are.' Hmmm, it's still comparatively easy to spot the bankers, disguised or otherwise: they're the ones claiming a vastly larger share of the pie, and then demanding the taxpayer compensates them for all the pies they've wastefully thrown away earlier; phew, satire!

Cycle Polo

Britain's upper and chav classes are basically the same: they both live on estates, keep scary dogs, are unnecessarily loud in public and possess an inexplicable fondness for Burberry clothing. Apart from the self-styled 'sport of commoners and kings' that horse racing believes it represents, sport actively barricades mobility between social classes by limiting informal class interaction. Polo is exclusively the protected preserve of the upper classes – and polo is the ultimate example of this seditious British class trait.

Previous attempts to remove the equine element from polo were typically Oxbridge, when the sport of Sedan Chair Polo was instigated. Really. Sedan Chair Polo: that's Oxford, keeping it real. Lady Margaret Hall undergraduate Nigella Lawson once participated in a game, inexpertly swinging a mallet while several hired irksome oiks transported her sedan chair around a makeshift polo field. This is so posh, the poshometer measuring poshness had to be recalibrated afterwards.

So it's good to report that polo has been hacked for the masses by Cycle Polo, where stabling fees are the cost of a bike lock. This particular sporting arena, this theatre of dreams, this stadium of light, is Curry's Superstore car park on the Botley Road retail park just off the A34. What I find particularly endearing about this sport – and I'd challenge you to think of many other competing examples elsewhere – is being left with an ambiguous impression as to whether they're officially allowed to be playing here. When was the last time you saw Manchester United's back four keeping a vigilant eye out in case the bloke who owned the ground came and moved them on for trespassing?

The game I witnessed was certainly fast-moving. Both sides initially cancelled each other out, with some alert defending. After a few minutes of tactical caution, players from each side became more ambitious in getting forward, and soon one team had a half chance to score. OK, maybe a quarter chance. But at least we'd witnessed our first shot at goal.

One player I conversed with was a delivery driver for an office paper supply company, but was planning to stand in local council elections – presumably due to his inspirational, 'I have a ream' speech. Actually proud of that one. Like several participants, he plays semi-regularly to keep both his physique and social life in good shape.

Another competitor revealed that he is a dedicated cyclist and planning a forthcoming cycle ride from Land's End to John O'Groats to raise money for charity; I immediately asked why he didn't plan to get the train instead, as that would surely allow him more time to raise money for charity once he got there? He didn't seem that grateful for the advice.

Cycle Polo is a lot older than it looks – originating in Ireland in the late nineteenth century. The Bicycle Polo Club of Great Britain printed the sport's rules in the *Morning Post* in 1898 and ensured the game was an official demonstration sport at the London 1908 Olympics. Having enjoyed sufficient participation to sustain a national league between the wars, British interest in the sport didn't return with the troops in 1945, leaving France, India, Canada and the US to dominate the world championships over the ensuing decades. But an enthusiastic group of mallet-waving pedallers ensures the sport continues in Britain today.

Annoyingly the Germans play Cycle Polo, and penalties are used to settle drawn matches; those two facts, while harmless in isolation, possess a potentially terrifying potency when combined. However, the French have always considered themselves invincible Cycle Polo experts, and are apparently still sensitively sore towards mentions of a famous English international victory in August 1939 when England defeated France 6–1. So we won't gloat. Six-une! Oh, we just did.

Dwile Flonking

To the uninitiated, untrained eye, Dwile Flonking appears to be a semi-sober rabble aimlessly hitting random bits of the countryside with wet sticks devoid of any apparent justifying reason. However, to the initiated, trained eye, Dwile Flonking appears to be a semi-sober rabble aimlessly hitting random bits of the countryside with wet sticks devoid of any apparent justifying reason.

The umpire is known as the 'jobanowl' and commences the game by shouting "ere ye go t'giher!' After dipping their flonking stick-tipped dwiles into a bucket of ale, this becomes known as a player's 'driveller'. With dwiles loaded, competitors must then toss the driveller in the direction of an opponent, scoring points if hitting them with his stale ale dish cloth. Opponents are referred to as 'girters', and must dance in a hand-holding circle around the flonker.

The inner circle constantly alternates between moving to the right and then back to the left – like Labour Party allegorists. However, should a miss occur, then a half-pint of ale must be downed as a forfeit. A match comprises of quartiles known as 'snurds' (which probably renders Dwile Flonking as a dual winner in the categories of both Silliest Game Ever and Best Sporting Terminology). Direct hits are worth 5 points (groin area), 3 points (head), 2 points (body) and 1 point (leg) and known, rather wonderfully, as an 'ouch', 'wanton', 'marther' and 'ripple' respectively. A complete miss is known as a 'swadger'.

After an hour and countless punitive half-pints knocked back, the formerly energetic stick-waving and flannel-chucking dissipates into general falling over without discernible justification nor objective. The consistent consumption of half-pints continues as it's apparently 'the rules'. After two hours, players wander without aim or purpose around East Anglian pub gardens, clubbing tufts of grass and unable to remember their dwile or home address. After three hours, someone, somehow, is declared a winner.

61

Winners compete for a chamber pot prize, which is inevitably filled with beer, since drinking is the core essence of the sport. Those taking part hold a flonking pole while supporting a soggy dwile on the end – 'dwile', in case you're wondering, derives from a Suffolk colloquialism for 'dish cloth', likely originating from the Dutch word for mop. The etymology of flonking is more open to dispute, but may be adapted from printers' terminology. This detail is seized on by some who claim the game was invented in the mid-1960s as merely a silly printers' apprenticeship ceremony, while others devoutly insist that the game is part of Suffolk and Norfolk's folklore, traceable all the way back to the early Middle Ages – though there is a troubling and inconvenient lack of any evidence for this latter view. Even the spelling is somewhat nebulous: some insist upon Dwyle Flunking.

The 2010 event was nearly scuppered by health and safety legislation – that stalking nemesis of Middle England – governing pubs' promotion of irresponsible binge drinking. In recent years the game has spread outside of East Anglia, with Sussex staging Dwile Flonking at the Lewes Arms – the same pub rightly famous for staging the annual Pea Throwing World Championship (see p. 100).

Gravy Wrestling
WORLD CHAMPIONSHIP

I know what you're probably thinking: less of a sport, more of a specialist website directing you to click that you're over 18 to enter. But this isn't quite what you may be expecting/gave your credit card number to access. It's not bored pretty girls in ludicrously small bikinis regretting not persevering with their GCSEs. It's wrestling, as in the noble Olympic Greco-Roman sport, muscular human pitched equally against muscular human in a battle of strength, tactics, undiluted aggression and who's got the boldest coloured lycra – having first just added water to the gravy granules. Cynics might interject

that the gravy part is unnecessary, and the sport of wrestling could function without it, but that would be a wholly different sport, and almost certainly one (let's call it 'wrestling') where the British wouldn't dominate as world champions.

Lancashire proudly hosts the event at the Rose 'N' Bowl pub in Stacksteads, equidistant between Burnley and Rochdale. The event certainly flexes its Lancashire pride, as well as wrestlers' developed muscles, and is probably not the correct environment to casually mention that a better use of gravy might be to accompany Yorkshire puddings rather than wrestlers.

The event raises money for a local hospice, and thankfully no one takes the gravy bouts seriously (if you don't like that pun, please skip the next sentence). Spectators attend from all over the north-west, travelling by gravy train, gravy boat and . . . (it's OK, I haven't got any more gravy transport references).

The pub landlady informed the local media, 'We normally have to make the gravy ourselves, which is a bit of a nightmare, but this year Bisto stepped in.' And 36 participants stepped in the Bisto, with Joel Hicks wrestling under the alias Stone Cold Steve Bisto, stepping out of the gravy to emerge as the world champion. That's another world champion for Britain. The women's event crowned Emma Slater – a 23-year-old from Oldham – world champion. She competed dressed as Mrs Christmas. She informed a BBC reporter, 'I didn't register until the last minute because I was only meant to be holding up the cards at the end of each round, so it has all come as a big surprise.'

As if to prove this event still hadn't reached the end of the crazy scale (pools filled with gravy, women dressed as Santa Claus in June, round card girls winning bouts . . . that's surely enough evidence), a large fire engine arrives, and the quickly dismounting crew proceed to discharge their water hoses at local wrestlers who have finished their bouts. Home and hosed in a very literal sense.

The Great Knaresborough Bed Race

The Great Knaresborough Bed Race provides, arguably ahead of all other sports featured in this book, a pitch-perfect combination of colourful fundraising fun with challenging sporting prowess. Hauling a cumbersome bed at speed over road and river is physically demanding, and teams can be seen training on local roads from early March.

The event recently celebrated Bob Chatten, whose unbroken participation in every race since 1974, proves you require good arms, good legs and a good

heart, given the event has always focused on raising money for charity. Volunteer organiser Nigel Perry confirms, 'for a third of the year the race is the main topic of conversation in the local pubs, and for us as volunteer organisers the task takes nine months.'

For a bunch of fun people pushing a bed around for charity, there are a lot of rules and regulations governing this event – it's organised with strict military precision, which becomes immensely less surprising once you become aware that the event was originated by the military and initially excluded civilians during its inaugural years. You can almost hear the throaty order, 'Stand by your beds!'

The course today retains its original 3km distance, which includes a dauntingly steep climb. Teams consist of six contestants – all over the age of twelve – while one team member must be in the bed at all times (students are probably an ideal choice for this role). Unlike other eccentric British sports (i.e. Wheelie Bin Racing), no swapping of personnel duties is

permitted. This explains a fecundity of pedantic rules – picking a rule at random: Rule 2 Sub-section F, Part (ix): 'Each team must have an audible air horn or hooter warning device but not a whistle.'

Some of these rules are serious – and they've kind of got a point with some, such as, 'All competitors must be able to swim for their own safety.' This is because a substantial section of the race occurs in the River Nidd. Paddling is not an option, as any teams optimistically anticipating a gentle wade realise that their feet are unlikely to be touching the ground again until they've crossed the river's murky waters. This may take place in June during the height of summer, but it is also in North Yorkshire, so the temperature could freeze the balls off a brassy Yorkshireman.

Infringement of any of the plethora of rules results in punishments ranging from incurring 30-second penalties (rare), through to a 2-minute time deduction for not being in regulation possession of ropes of less than 3.76 metres attached to the bed, up to disqualification and expulsion from all future events.

The race is a marvellous spectacle, combining athleticism, strength, speed, stamina and wonderful British eccentricity. Nigel Perry perceptively opines: 'It looks like lots of fun, but in that very Yorkshire sort of way you wouldn't know from most of the racers, for whom it is highly competitive and very gritty. As it has been going for forty-six years, there are full grown Crag Rats (Knaresborians born and bred) who know of little else.'

The Great Shirt Race

Supposedly named after an item of bedwear long since transposed by the transience of fashion: the night shirt. Inaugurated in 1953 – yes, the year is significant as patriotic citizens of Bampton in Oxfordshire wished to honour the Queen's coronation by, er, conducting a massive pub crawl in their pyjamas. And here's the really clever bit (for 'clever' I do of course mean 'dumb') – devising wheel-based mobility with exemption from drink/driving prosecution. OK, that is quite clever.

Teams usually comprise three (or two in the youths' race), with regulations requiring one stipulated rider/driver to be transported on a homemade 'vehicle' while his/her team-mates pull, push, heave or generally shove them around the course. The course consists of eleven pubs – well, it did in 1953, but with over fifty pubs a week in the UK ringing the last orders bell for the final time, it is perhaps unsurprising to discover that Bampton now only has four remaining public houses. Not to worry, as resourceful community-minded locals merely resurrect the ghosts of deceased pubs with a drinks table temporarily erected outside the buildings once occupied by the former inns – hence three former pubs were returned as beverage providers for one evening each year. There is also a youths' Great Shirt Race, where some of the youngsters travel at a pace akin to Jeremy Clarkson passing a recently decommissioned speed camera, as they recklessly hurtle along Bampton's streets as fleetingly recognisable blurs – though they are forced to consume strictly non-alcoholic beverages en route.

Keen to convey the impression that the Great Shirt Race is not merely a nebulous pub crawl, a noble attempt is made by volunteer officials to enforce unenforceable rules such as participants mustn't spill drinks to save time and avoid inevitable inebriation.

Each adult competitor must be observed by judges to down a beer at each of the designated stops (half measures permitted for the ladies – though I saw at least one woman evidently so uncomfortable with such sexist concessions that she downed a full pint instead), especially since organisers have provided the very best kind of beer: free beer. Teams compete in regulation fancy dress, and there's a refreshing attitude towards refreshment displayed by some teams, who prefer lingering for a drink and a chat in the pubs en route, to the inconvenience of troublesome racing.

The money raised pays for the town's 430 pensioners to attend an annual outing and enables them to receive a £20 Christmas present; this, unquestionably, is a good thing. A unique and distinctive event that provides fun, colour and a forged social identity for this pleasant small Oxfordshire town; long may it continue.

Gurning
WORLD CHAMPIONSHIPS

Presumably due to Cumbria's persistent lack of success with mainstream sports (they're not in cricket's County Championship, their Cartmel horse racing course was Britain's least utilised and once ran through someone's back garden and their only Football League team, Carlisle United, recently spent several years annexed in the non-league game), they've decided to invent their own sport. And you can't say they haven't been successful at this sport, although it's not necessarily a pretty sight.

As is proven annually on the third Saturday in September when Egremont hosts the World Gurning Championship, and usually accommodates attracted TV news crews. There are separate men's, children's and women's categories – the latter being the unofficial Miss Ugly to the official (or officially anachronistic) Miss World.

The event claims to have origins in the thirteenth century, when King Henry granted a Royal Charter in 1266 to stage a fair in the area. Face-pullers wear a 'braffin' – that's horse collar to you and me – and then conduct the serious business of becoming as ugly as possible. The sport is as toothless as a voluntary code of conduct, with winners usually being contestants without any teeth (it allows far greater freedom for facial expression). The sport's best known (heavily distorted) face was probably Peter Jackman who won the event on four occasions and appeared in the 'Feel The Sportsman' round on BBC1's snidey panel comedy *They Think It's All Over*.

Gurning is free to enter though it may cost you your dignity.

Haxey Hood

Lincolnshire. Whichever direction you look, everywhere is ironed flat: creaselessly and uncompromisingly flat – the landscape locked in compelling uneventful nothingness, everything perpetually destined to be played out under a vast, endless melancholic sky. The Haxey Hood occurs in the north of the county, in an area collectively known as the swampy Isle of Axholme (an unlikely lone bit of Lincolnshire that confusingly sits on the western side of the River Trent), though the game's probable founder John de Mowbray was from North Yorkshire rather than North Lincolnshire. As the 3rd Baron of Mowbray, he pursued an active role in battle in 1346. Several thousand troops on horseback engaged in the Battle of Neville's Cross (estimated at approaching 20,000 combatants), but history doesn't record whether Neville was successful in keeping his cross. It does, however, record that combat commenced when a Scottish raiding party arrived fresh from invading northern England while Edward was away deploying a similar plan to invade northern France – who in turn were fighting the Spanish to their south.

The Scots sacked Hexham priory and castle. As any military strategist would know, the weakest part of a fortified castle, and thus the part most vulnerable to enemy attack, is always the gift shop. Within a week they were marching towards the prize of Durham, yet in spite of being outnumbered almost 3 to 1, they were repelled by the English. Yorkshireman John de Mowbray was rewarded with land in north-west Lincolnshire. When his wife rode out on this gifted land one windy afternoon in about 1350, her bonnet was blown away and was eventually recouped by a toiling peasant following a chase across nearby fields. Legend recounts he was too hideously repressed by the class serfdom system to return it directly to Lady Mowbray – so she insensitively branded him 'a Fool', but a bolder peasant, presumably less subjugated by the feudal system, did approach Her Ladyship directly, and handed back the windswept bonnet.

Realising a grand gesture was required, Lady Mowbray decreed that 13 acres of land would be granted to the local peasants upon condition that the chase for her hood should be restaged every year. That's what the aristocracy have always done well in this country: mad pointless gestures demonstrating their ostentatious wealth to assembled grateful doffers. Unlike most promises made by rich to poor, this one was never reneged. Unanimous local opinion believes the game has been conducted ever since the peasant's chivalrous act prompted Lady Mowbray to invent the

game, though the only bonnets visible in today's game are a few dented ones on foolishly parked cars – in recent years players have trampled cars into something akin to a one-dimensional metal sheet. This is also a hazard for spectators, as the game can appear stationary for prolonged periods, only for the scrum to break free, resulting in the pack (known as 'The Sway') comprising numerous muscular men in straining XXXL rugby shirts pumped with adrenalin and alcohol coursing through their veins, hurtling straight towards you.

Watched by a huge attendance in freezing conditions, the Haxey Hood is traditionally staged on 'Old Christmas Day' on the shivering 6 January. The Hood is fought over by four pubs in Haxey and nearby Westwoodside (Duke William, Loco, Carpenter's Arms, The Kings – all of whom opt to protect their floors with heavy-duty polythene from muddy, bloody rugger-buggers) for the right to keep it behind their bar for the next twelve months. Throwing and kicking (either the hood or opponents) is not allowed. Indeed, the Hood can only be moved

collectively by The Sway. Umpires struggling to control proceedings are known locally as 'Boddins', supervised by a 'Lord of the Hood'.

Various tactical machinations are deployed; culminating in one year's game when a suspiciously easy passage of play for one team suddenly ended with a planned ambush by a rival pub once they'd passed a concealing wall.

Before the game commences, the Fool stands aloft an improvised plinth in front of the church, and clutching the leather cylinder in one hand, makes a speech – his voice sufficiently sharp to pierce through the thick winter mist. Soon a populous scrum of charity world record attempt proportions assembles. The problem with giant rugby scrums involving over 100 people are manyfold (apart from the obvious concern that people trapped in the middle probably died an hour ago) is that the Hood disappears from spectator and player view for prolonged periods.

Steam rises from the heaving masses both figuratively and literally, resembling the mighty pressure and power of a steam engine impatiently awaiting a signal to turn green. When one side eventually re-emerges dominant with possession and moves through the Lincolnshire fields, it provides a glimpse of the engine's power. Bursts of steam rise from those capable of emerging upright from the scrum unaided. But all too soon it's stuck at another red light of stalemate as rival villagers catch up. Finally, The Sway moves again and eventually reaches one of the four pubs ascribed to the game – the landlady is standing on the doorstep. The Hood's grabbed, and once moved to safety, proclaimed as the trophy it is. Once this stage has been reached, all the day's earlier drinking is demonstrated as comparative palate-cleansing, compared to the real drinking that is now about to commence.

Horseball

orseball sounds self-explanatory – certainly when compared to sports such as Dwile Flonking and Aunt Sally. Invented in the early eighteenth century in Argentina, Horseball is a mongrel amalgamation of polo, basketball and rugby: polo without sticks, basketball without hoops, and rugby without a fat bloke gouging your eye out. Nowadays the ball (an adapted size 4 soccer ball) contains six handles, aiding players who ride like Cossacks into battle, stooping down low to gain possession by picking up the ball. Unfortunately, the 'ball' was formerly a duck. And as if this has the capacity to get any worse: it was a live duck.

Yet it wasn't only ducks dying horrendous and premature deaths. Argentina formally banned Horseball in 1790 when the authorities saw the ridiculously high human mortality rates. Later the game was introduced to Europe, and became crossbred with an infused Gallic influence after the French authorities requested in the early 1970s that a countryman invent a sport that the whole of France could play. A modified and revamped Horseball was the winning entry, which is odd for many reasons, but here's two: (a) it assumes everyone in the entire country keeps horses, and (b) if the French are going to be using their horses for this newly adapted Horseball sport, then what's for lunch tomorrow?

However, priding ourselves on being a somewhat horsey nation, the British have become involved and aim to feature as a prominent force in the world game: the phrase 'world game' in this context mainly meaning France and Argentina, augmented

by a few minor countries like, ahem, Canada, Brazil and the US. OK, so there are a few more European ones too (Portugal and Spain are considered to be effective Horseball outfits, and have won European Championships). The advantage of Britain playing a competitive sport internationally that has limited participation among an exclusive number of nations, ought to ensure a high probability of success.

Horseball teams comprise four horses and four humans and the game has two halves of 10 minutes. Goals are approximately 1 metre in diameter, yet suspended from a 12ft high pole. Ingeniously, rules only permit players to pick up the ball from the ground if they are following the direction of play i.e. this convincingly decreases the likelihood of head-on collisions (that would be less like Horseball, more like jousting), and sudden horse 'braking'. Two umpires, dressed in the official American sports tradition of black and white striped jerseys, attempt to keep order over a surprisingly physical game, with origins visibly imported from rugby. Players can be tackled in possession, and top equine skills are required, given a successful player must virtually ride a horse hands-free. There's an active British Horseball Association and, crucially, we're already better than the Germans.

Korfball

Indigenous British sports need to be adaptable if they are to survive a European challenger. Korfball invaded these shores comparatively recently yet the sport has expanded aggressively throughout the UK in quick time – like the grey squirrel of eccentric British sports – and thus presumably earned the hostility of the *Daily Mail* in the process. Korfball has been rapidly adopted by the British, recognising that it may have more to offer than netball and bottle-kicking, because here is a game finally capable of dismantling the gender divide that remains structurally sound in several twenty-first-century sports. All other areas of human existence seem to have successfully implemented a progressive gender democracy where men and women are equally capable of doing any job side by side, yet sport still appears unready. Netball needs to accept men can play it too. And that mixed games can happen. Doesn't it, netball? Or Korfball will become bigger than you.

I can exclusively reveal that Formula One Motor Racing is only the second loudest sport. Korfball is played against a backdrop of constant, uninterrupted screaming. Screaming frequently ascends in tonal pitch to screeching. I suspect there is also a higher frequency sound, judging by a nearby dog attempting to stick his front paws into his ears.

Korfball has enjoyed a recent spike in British interest. Teams consist of four men and four women, with half the team permitted free-range roaming – though four players must stay in their half of a 40m x 20m court, and not transgress the half-way line. Knee and ankle injuries are common as players avoid straight-line running in an attempt to avoid markers. Korfball cleverly insures itself against the British climate by being played both indoors and outdoors. Like netball and basketball, it is a non-contact sport. Korfball's eccentricity exists from being thoroughly gender engendered. And its mad baskets.

Korfball's legitimacy as an eccentric sport – and thus enthusiastic adoption by the British – lies in its name: the 'korf' in korfball is the Dutch word for 'basket' – or 'waste basket'! They are traditionally made of wicker (though plastic now pervades), and it does look decidedly odd to see players attempting to put the ball into a bin.

Eight Korfball World Championships have been held, with Holland and Belgium occupying the winner and runner-up positions in all eight tournaments! Britain came closest to breaking this Benelux monopoly in 1987 when they claimed the bronze medal.

Lawnmower Racing

There's an old joke: why do women need men? Because vibrators can't mow the lawn. Nowadays they are increasingly unlikely to mow the lawn either, since men are requisitioning the garden mower for the emerging sport of lawnmower racing. The lawnmower racing season runs from May to October, and includes a British Grand Prix at Silverstone, World Championship and a Le Mans-style Twelve Hour Endurance Race; all of which faithfully mirrors the traditional motorsport season – apart from the constant stops to empty the grass box.

Branded by the *Kentish Times* as 'enjoyable insanity' – which is the most accurate description possible if permitted only two words – lawnmower racing was founded in 1973. Fittingly, the sport was born at the maternity hospital where so many eccentric sports were delivered into the world: a pub. Jim Gavin was in the Cricketers Arms in Wisborough Green, West Sussex, bemoaning the decaying influence of sponsorship and spiking inflation on traditional motor racing, when he noticed the village green being cut outside, and decided to organise a mower race in a nearby field. After rejecting other new motorsports (according to the British Lawnmower Museum motorised bar-stools were soon overlooked as being passé), lawnmower racing was settled upon. Unsure as to how many would turn up for the inaugural event in 1973, it turned out that no fewer than eighty men went to mow a meadow. Though dogs aren't allowed.

The British Lawn Mower Racing Association now oversees the sport, and racing-approved lawnmowers receive a unique chassis stamp to adduce their legality. The sport certainly involves cutting edge technology (sorry). Although overseeing all rules, regulations and practices, none of the sport's practitioners seem sure whether lawn mower/ lawnmower is one word or two. A former lawnmower racing champion curates the British Lawnmower Museum in wide-boulevarded Southport; exhibits thrillingly displayed in the celebrity's lawnmower section genuinely include Joe Pasquale's strimmer!

Britain has been provided with yet another world record, thanks to eccentric sports, when Don Wales hit 87.83mph (and thankfully no hard objects) claiming the lawnmower land speed record in 2010 at Pendine Sands in Carmarthenshire, claiming the record from Australia. Lawnmower record attempters must demonstrate grass-cutting to judges, and use a mower initially bought as a bona fide lawnmower to receive world record eligibility. Appropriately, Don's grandfather Sir Malcolm Campbell broke the world land speed record (sans lawnmower) at the same location in 1924.

Not many world championships occur in rural Wiltshire, yet the Heddington and Stockley Steam Rally hosts this lawnmowing event of global significance. Again, the emphasis is on authenticated lawnmowers that were primarily designed for, and are still able to reproduce upon official inspection, their original grass-cutting capabilities.

The sport has ascended in popularity recently, helped by several 'news in brief' newspaper stories – they must have a busy press officer, since there are clippings everywhere. (Clippings! See what I did there!? . . . oh suit yourself).

Men's Netball

It's early. Before 6 a.m. early. Aggressively early. And given that I'm with a bunch of students, where early constitutes any time before *Countdown* starts, then this is off-the-scale, uncharted early. As a rule, there aren't many sporting events that start this early; but we're suspending all the rules today. Because the participants don't want spectators. It's a clandestine event, stealthily orchestrated below the publicity radar. The participants I'm travelling with turn off their engine well ahead of the venue – they don't want the deep roar of engine noise to awake locals and attract suspicion. Participants are already changed, removing their civilian clothes to reveal the outfits that signal their sport: tight lobster bibs adorned with capital letters such as 'GA'. Welcome to the unashamed world of Men's netball. And no one's prepared to talk 'on camera'.

For some reason, people recoil in horror whenever you prefix the word 'netball' (a perfectly harmless, acceptable and healthy word) with 'Men's'. It's like putting the word 'ITV' before 'sitcom', or 'Chancellor' before 'George Osborne'.

England netball's website publicises their Goalden Globe Awards (they're so punny), which provide recognition for worthy causes. Nothing inherently wrong or funny about that. Until you read that the awards are for disadvantaged 'groups' e.g. disabled people, disadvantaged communities, men and boys'.

Netball is a hugely popular British sport. And yet, mysteriously, 50 per cent of the population possess no concept of how it's done – like hopscotch and an innate ability to wear a towel as a post-bath turban. So why can one of Britain's most popular sports be transformed into an eccentric sport just by adding the prefix 'Men's'? Why this sporting apartheid?

I court responses: 'men's netball? Er, unnatural,' being one depressingly common reaction. However, Greg, attending the dawn training session, is prepared to elaborate, as long as I don't reveal his surname (!), 'My girlfriend plays, and she got me into it. Instead of just watching her play, I wanted to get involved. People think that's odd, but I tell them I get to hang around with a group of gorgeous girls, and then everyone seems to think it's a great idea.' Er, everyone with the possible exception of your girlfriend, Greg.

Greg elaborates: 'Most men can't seem to think past the sexual connotations of hanging around with a team of women. Which is bizarre.'

'Primitive,' I interject.

'Yeah, exactly. They make stupid jokes about it.'

I decide not to orate the stupid joke I was about to make.

'Plenty of blokes work with women in offices, but people don't make them endure stupid comments like "bet you spend all day in the stationery cupboard with your girls?".'

Greg is clearly one of the good guys, who volunteers considerable free time for his genuine enthusiasm towards the sport, and he wants men's participation in netball to become much more popular. Although his team lose, they're clearly well organised.

Men's netball differs from women's netball – it's quieter. Surprisingly women's netball is louder than rugby too; rugby has grunting and consistent snap of tendons and gnawing of ears, but some female netball teams I've seen would terrify the All Blacks into abandoning the Haka half-performed.

Netball is an ideal game for a mixed social sport. For a non-contact sport it is surprisingly fast-paced and physical; fitness levels need to be high and regularly topped up, though the game's zonal restraints (players cannot leave set areas) are an unnecessary barrier of rigidity. Yet it remains inexplicable how the basketball = men, netball = women apartheid orthodoxy evolved. Unjustly, netball (of any gender variant) remains snubbed by the Olympics.

Monopoly
WORLD CHAMPIONSHIPS

Prophetic in its single-minded vision that one day all utility companies would be privatised, Monopoly continues to enjoy resurging interest in the twenty-first century while annually retaining its number one position as the world's most unfinished game. When Charles Darrow invented the board game in Depression-era America (most people consider it British – it's not, although Britain was hugely influential in shaping the game's

current format), taking 3–4 hours in an evening or unemployed afternoon was fine, even when one guy (and there's always one player who does this) insists on counting out the money v-e-r-y s-l-o-w-l-y before pronouncing the shatteringly unoriginal comment, 'hey, wouldn't it be great if all this money was real?'

After spending several hours constantly going around in circles – or, more accurately, squares – enduring insights such as, 'that'll cost you £13,' and, 'oh, £300 is cheap for Oxford Street – I wouldn't mind buying it for that' – you can see why *The Young Ones* livened up Monopoly by amending Chance cards to read 'Smash Rick over the head with box lid.' Unfortunately, Rick, Vyvyan and Neil's Monopoly reimaginings have often proved better than the real thing: Monopoly has issued licences to seemingly almost every request for a version of the game. Sometimes this has been done well (*The Simpsons* version actually contains some traceable effort and imagination in the redesign) while other franchises look like they were written during an advert break in *Coronation Street*. It is, by the way, possible to buy a *Coronation Street* version of the game.

Monopoly can also offer what most of Middle England truly courts: free parking. But it can't offer a recent British world champion, even though the game has a strongly forged association with Britain. Let's ask a question: which city is featured on the original American version of Monopoly? Did you go for New York? Me too. But the correct answer is Atlantic City, and this obscure choice was identified as an early problem by a then moderately successful Leeds-based card printer named Waddingtons. Company director Victor Watson decided to create a version that featured London, and researched thematic streets for the game's colour-coded blocks (i.e. Bow, Vine and Marlborough Street are connected by their association with law). It's worth recalling that the British version was being researched before the American equivalent had yet gone into production, so the game's popularity was still an unknown risk. Charles Darrow sold royalty rights to Monopoly for an egregiously small fee, reportedly declining an offer for individual royalties over a one-off fee.

First contested in New York in 1973, the world championship is held every two years, with the victor collecting a cash prize of $20,580 – if you consider that an unusually specific amount, that's because it is the accrued total of the cash in a monopoly set. The latest British Championship was settled over four tournaments held in Birmingham, Bournemouth, Skegness and Blackpool – and heavily promoted with the tag line 'British Monopoly: from Birmingham to Bond Street'. The British winner was sent to contest the world championship in Las Vegas that was eventually won by a Norwegian, nineteen-year-old Bjorn Knappskog.

The Angel, Islington: the only property on the Monopoly board to be named after a building.

Mountain Bike Chariot

WORLD CHAMPIONSHIPS

Let's role play for a moment. Go on, it'll be fun. Right, you are responsible for organising the World Mountain Bike Chariot Championships in secluded – and, as the name implies – mountainous woodland. In Wales. What would be the optimum time to stage this event for competitors and spectators alike in this notoriously wet and cold country? That's right. You've chosen January. And you're sacked. Hang on, no you've got the job – as that turns out to be the correct answer. January. In Wales. In the forest. Are. You. Having. A. Laugh?

The rain is relentless. Just as you conclude that there cannot be any water left in the atmosphere to fall, the rain actually becomes momentarily harder. By the latter races, only a rider's helmet is visibly raised above the mud – and that's because they're the one standing upright in the chariot; there's no sign of his other two team members. Puddles are rapidly expanding into lakes; herons swoop down into the puddle/lake in the track and ascend with a fish. Moments later a cyclist and chariot both disappear into the puddle/lake. A worrying few seconds pass as bubbles rise to the surface, and then they're pulled out. Then it starts to rain much harder. A contestant, without apparent awareness of irony, purchases a bottle of water for £1 – although currently standing in probably the largest reserve of free water in the world; anyone who pays for bottled water is so Evian spelled backwards.

The world championship is decided by a series of heats throughout the day, when teams of three compete against each other on the woodland circuit. Resources are split into two pedalling riders pulling a third team member who must remain in the chariot i.e. falling out and hurting themselves badly is against the rules. Phew. Although it may occasionally happen due to ridiculously optimistic cornering speeds deployed by some of the novice teams. The person in the chariot is not issued with a whip, although some mime whip use, while others utilise the adequate

surrogate of their tongue to get the inept twin cyclists to pedal faster. If the chariot looks more like an adapted dustbin than a chariot, then that's because it probably is a dustbin.

There are inevitably narrow parts of the track, and overtaking can lead to hazardous wheel locking – although blades are mercifully not permitted on the chariot wheels (for all the praise lavished upon Roman pioneering administrative techniques and progressive order, the Roman Empire's Health and Safety department was seriously lax).

The route passes the beckoning, winking lights of a warm dry pub – which during the rain-lashed, wind-whipped, perpetual darkness of indistinguishable day and night that was the 2011 world championship, ensures a necessary stubborn resolve from teams wanting to collect that coveted (and wet) world championship trophy. Nevertheless, ten teams competed in the worst Welsh weather for the prize.

Fancy dress, often with an appropriate Roman theme, is seemingly mandatory. One team made ingenious use of red broom heads to convincingly accessorise their Roman helmets. Fittingly, one competitor arranged a toga party for fellow chariot racers that evening – which was fortunate since bed sheets from the B&B would be the only dry clothing available to most people after enduring a January day in Wales.

The event is bookended by the two-day Roman food and drink festival Saturnalia, which takes its name from the Roman God Saturn who was honoured with a winter festival – hence it's entirely his fault that this takes place in January.

Llanwrtyd Wells, which hosts the world championships, has a population of 600 and a claim on being the smallest town in Britain. Protected by the surrounding Cambrian Mountains, the area offers an impressive, imposing natural beauty for those involved in, or merely observing, the action.

Nettle Eating

WORLD CHAMPIONSHIPS

ave you the mettle for the nettle? Held in the eighteenth-century Bottle Inn in the Dorset village of Marshwood near Bridport, competitors must remove the leaves from numerous 2ft-long nettle stalks and, er, eat them. Ouch.

The air is electric. That's because there's a thunderstorm brewing, rather than any great sporting atmosphere. The one thing you can't remove from the atmosphere is the sting. In fact, the atmosphere is perhaps fairly described as anxious rather than joyous, with an unspoken feeling of regret commonly hosted by several participants, as the actuality of what they drunkenly signed up to undertake several weeks earlier becomes a sober reality: namely eating stinging nettles.

Some, already taking their seats on the raised platform before a table of long fresh nettles, are seized by oppressive doubts, and visibly contemplate making a dash for the green-lit fire door even at this late stage. Chatting with spectators, a few recount that previous participants have remarked, 'oh, I've left my sunglasses in the car,' and were then seen driving out of the car park with squealing acceleration, never to return.

'Yeah,' adds George (not his real name for reasons you're about to fathom), 'it's the classic man-losing-his-nerve-when-visiting-a-brothel excuse.' That's probably opened up a window into George's private life we'd preferred had remained curtained.

There's an awkward silence while everyone takes a sip of their drink.

'You don't have to swallow the seeds,' says another spectator, 'but you have to eat all the leaves, but not the stem, obviously.'

'Doesn't it make you seriously ill?' I ask with concern.

'Not if you're sufficiently pissed.'

Being held at a pub does have benefits, as many participants choose to drink ale to aid digestion and anaesthetise the pain. Smarter competitors roll the leaves into balls, and then throw them towards the back of the throat for minimum mouth exposure. World record holder Simon Sleigh of Hawkchurch munched his way through 76ft of stinging nettles, and charmingly informed the *Daily Telegraph* afterwards, 'everything comes out green for several days.' Shiver. However, any nettle-eater visiting the toilet during the allocated one hour of the contest will receive an automatic disqualification. Judges also monitor excess waste – even dribble is measured by exasperated officials. All nettles are now supplied by the pub, sourced locally by the judges, as in previous years mendacious extra-acidic nettle swapping was rumoured to have occurred.

Capped at sixty-five entrants, the event regularly attracts nearly 1,000 spectators to the pub where it started in 1986 when local Alex Williams arrived possessing both a 14ft-long nettle and an erroneous confidence that this constituted the longest nettle in Dorset. Challenging anyone to produce a longer nettle, he unwisely pledged to eat his own 14-footer should that surely incontrovertible, unassailable truth not be beholden. Later that same evening, he ate his 14-footer. Another drinker, supposedly without having to endure the inconvenience of leaving the village, produced a longer specimen and the contest was born.

Occasionally the championship is tied, with two contestants sharing the 2010 world championship title. Neither could eat beyond 48ft of nettles (which sounds like a reasonable enough sentence).

Contestants have an hour to consume the stinging greenery, with enforced rules stating that they cannot expel nettles; this was unpleasantly illustrated one year when a participant, moments from victory, treated the pub garden to the recoiling sight of his body rejecting the previous 58 minutes of consumed nettles in an enormous technicolour (well, mainly green) yawn.

Onion Eating

W O R L D   C H A M P I O N S H I P

ere comes the science bit: the reason for onion-peeling inducing crying akin to a melodramatic soap death is due to sulphuric acid being released once the onion's protective membrane has been severed. Hence attempting to eat half a pound of onions in under 2 minutes is equivalent to drinking a fresh onion smoothie in one. An eye-watering fact whichever way you look at it (though mainly through blurry, teary eyes) and more acidic than the tone of a letter from the bank addressing an unauthorised overdraft.

However, those with burning ambitions and desires (and later, throats) assemble in Newent, Gloucestershire, each August to contest the national championship. I say 'national', they say 'the world', as they somewhat understandably doubt whether other countries would register sufficient insanity to stage such a contest. But it transpires there are. And when it comes to internationally competitive bad breath, our closest onion-munchers are predictably the French.

But the French onion is subtly different, as their French onion soup testifies. Go one country further south from France, and again the national onion transforms: the Spanish onion providing the connoisseur with an even subtler, milder taste. So it's certainly an event where you need to know your onions.

It turns out that Britain usually supplies the winner at the contest held since 1996 in the town's market square as part of the wider, and much older, Newent Onion Fayre that supposedly originated in the thirteenth century. Contestants sit behind a platform table. Men have to eat through an eye-watering 7oz onion, while the women's contest decrees the onion must weigh no less than 5oz. This is potentially one of the fastest world championships in sport after the 100m sprint final, given the event is usually measured in seconds rather than minutes. However, with a festival wholly dedicated to the bulbous majesty of the onion occurring alongside the contest, there is plenty for attendees to enjoy on a pleasant day out.

Hopefully Newent's shops have the foresight to stock extra-strong breath mints.

Pantomime Horse Grand National

There are innumerable imponderables in the world. What will Ann Widdecombe do when her looks go? Why is there a Salvation Army but no Salvation Navy or Air Force? What do pantomime horses do for the eleven months of the year when there's a dearth of pantomimes? Well, the last question can now be definitively answered – they train for the Pantomime Horse Grand National.

Each November pantomime horses assemble in Birmingham city centre. Oh yes they do. Billed as the ultimate way to decide who is the fastest horse to clear a course of straw bale fences, instead competitors with a natural proclivity for showbiz sight gags are rewarded with the warmest audience appreciation. One 'horse' makes no attempt to jump any fence, instead creating huge laughter whenever he plunges straight into a fence with spectacular slapstick physicality and consequences.

It's all unimpeachably worthwhile, raising money for the Lord Mayor's charity appeal towards funding a local hospital, and everyone acts like they're aware it's a joke (an attitude which, if imported into conventional horse racing, may risk significantly improving it).

That said, it's not just horsing about, as the 500-metre course can be surprisingly gruelling – especially when you're dressed as a horse.

Pantomime horses come with driver/operator jockeys adorned with colourful silks and caps, who must steer their steeds over (or more often, through) twelve straw bale fences. There is also a boys' (colts) and girls' (fillies) race; though organisers presumably counselled against calling the women's category 'mares'.

In 2009 the female race was won by Nicki Mills, riding the superbly named Spank The Donkey and thus magnificently managing to simultaneously offend both prudes and animal rights activists.

Entrants for the 500-metre race are attracted from around the country (a Devonian jumped to glory recently on his 'horse' Hoof Hearted) and pay £50, with the annual British Pantomime Grand National winner bagging a bottle of champagne: so a definite loss on their investment – like most people's experience of a day at the races – but this one is entirely for good causes.

The event started in 2002, and attracts sizeable crowds to central Birmingham, even when the temperature risks freezing the thermometer mercury as it did in a shivering November Grand National in 2010 – though some locals continue shopping, deliberately oblivious to the spectacle of human horses and the cluttered colours of jockeys' silks, evidently thinking 'nothing unusual worth distracting me from shopping here.' There most certainly is.

Pea Shooting
WORLD CHAMPIONSHIPS

r Whottle was my school maths teacher. I remember him (he was a wise man), and I'll wager that he remembers me, mainly because I was 100 per cent awful at maths. After leaving school, I've often contemplated why I was 100 per cent appalling at maths, and concluded that it must be because I am 50 per cent lazy, 50 per cent inattentive and 50 per cent innumerate. He told me, not unreasonably, that I was the worst maths student he had personally encountered in his professional career. That remark would not have been so damaging had it been his first day after leaving teacher training college, yet it was sagely orated to a nodding class just before his retirement after fifty loyal years facing the blackboard. Years later I saw him at a football match, and he did indeed remember me for being the worst ever maths student.

'So, what career did you go into?' he enquired with genuine interest.

'Actuary, sir,' I lied. Then I suddenly remembered, 'Mr Whottle, could I have my pea shooter back that you confiscated in 1978?' Turns out he didn't have it on him.

Fast forward several years and I'm now standing in Ely in 2011 – struggling to work out if I've been given the right change in a pub and bemoaning my inattentive wastefulness during Mr Whottle's lessons. Eventually I succeed, and conclude that the change the cashier handed me was completely 101 per cent correct.

Ironically, the Pea Shooting World Championship was started by a schoolteacher: John Tyson inaugurated the contest in 1971, rendering the 2011 event held on an early July sunny Saturday, the . . .

er . . . I'll definitely get this . . . add 4 . . . got it . . . competition's fiftieth anniversary. OK, sixtieth then? fortieth! Definitely the fortieth. I did get quite proficient at pea shooting during those classes, though possibly neglected mathematics.

Several competitors have assembled in the village of Witcham, irregularly served by the X9 bus from nearby Ely. I ask in the White Horse pub if the village is buzzing with world championship fever; one guy doesn't think so, pronouncing his intention to remain drinking all day. He misses an international field, with a few Americans taking part alongside a large local turnout. Accuracy is key, as pea puffers must shoot their minuscule green projectiles against targets pinned to hay bales distanced 12ft from the oche. The highest scoring 16 competitors qualify for a knockout stage, culminating in the final where both participants shoot ten peas to determine the highest score.

Should you dismiss pea shooting as ultimately mere luck, then take participatory inspiration from the story of nearby Haddenham resident Ian Ashmeade who finished second in 2009 after picking up a pea shooter for the first time on the eve of the contest, yet returned triumphant in 2010 to go one place better. They've got to make a movie – they just have to.

Over the years, the event has raised sufficient money to build a new village hall. So, pea shooting did turn out to be more useful than maths. It should be taught in schools.

Pea Throwing
WORLD CHAMPIONSHIP

'Do you want peas?' the chip shop proprietor asks. 'They're half price with fish orders today 'cos of the event.'

'Yeah, please – seems appropriate for today.' A ladle of mushy green slime is then dismissively splodged onto a polystyrene tray. Departing the chippy, I head for the World Pea Throwing Championship. It's not a case of following the crowds, as there aren't any. The action takes place along a side street in Lewes, East Sussex. Lewes is not unlike Monte Carlo – i.e. once a year the place is transformed from bustling town to sporting arena; OK, they close a small side street for 20 minutes.

Then the peas are menacingly drawn. Within a few seconds of the start, an obvious spectator peril becomes evident: beware flying peas. This is because they are invisible in flight, given they're the size of a, well, pea. And any sport that is mainly invisible renders a limitation on spectator appeal.

Squinting my eyes in anticipation of a pea strike that never happens, I hear screams of others confirming they weren't so fortunate. There is also the occasional 'that's not my pea!' to the measuring judges, whereas they point to another indistinguishable pea – always further away, of course – that they manifestly affirm was shot from their palm. In truth it regularly approaches chaos, but the result is a good-humoured situation, not a freefall towards a sporting dystopia, with

officials diligently ensuring the correct measurements are recorded. Here's a tip organisers can have for free next year: issue different coloured peas. Should competitors be given peas dyed different colours, then judging differentiation would be rendered newly possible.

A refractory teenager claims that his pea has been hurled the furthest, a proclamation that the judges correctly opt to take with a pinch of salt. After numerous frantic tape measuring, a winner is eventually declared.

Staged annually in Lewes at the Lewes Arms, participants have three throws each. The world record stood at a mightily impressive 38.7m, thrown by Danny Tear in 2003, yet this was eclipsed by a 43m chuck in 2009. Should you be wondering if he produced a golf ball spray-painted green seconds before lobbing it past fleetingly distracted judges, then the answer is unlikely as the pub's judges claim to strictly adjudicate and invigilate each individual pea to ensure size and weight consistency. And it's probably the cheapest sport possible to pursue, democratically welcoming participants of all ages and wages, genders and agendas. So, far from being a pea-brained operation, then.

Pie Eating
WORLD CHAMPIONSHIP

Here's a common scene repeated in many doctors' surgeries. After an initial consultation, a GP solemnly asks if their patient has considered taking up a sporting pursuit, and prompts them to suggest a sport they may like to adopt. Well, here's a good answer to offer your GP: competitive pie eating.

Predilection for pies? Proclivity for sports? Why not combine the two – after all, there's exercise to be had here: those wrappers don't come off the pie by themselves, and you have to chew (although winning competitors dispense with the chewing – takes too much effort and thus compromises your net calories gain).

Daring to deviate from the sport's (and the area's) unwavering conviction that a pie should contain

nothing but meat and potato or risk no longer being a pie – believing otherwise is sufficient to fail a normality test in Wigan – a vegetarian pie was liberally permitted in the official rules in 2006. Modernisers also succeeded in implementing a crucial alteration to the competition, by changing the outcome from the cumulative number of pies consumed in three minutes to gorging just one solitary pie against the clock; Tony Callaghan, 2006 world champion, informed the *Guardian*, 'I realise it may be controversial, but this is the way forward for pie eating at this level.'

In more recent times the sport has visibly reduced its Northernness, and made several concessions to modernity: quoffing their cloth caps to vegetarianism, tidying up their cobbled yards, clearing out their pigeon sheds, and putting their whippets on a lead – literally in the latter case, given the 2007 event was nearly destroyed by an organiser's dog eating several of the event's pies before the competition started (luckily the dog ran off, or that year's victor Anthony 'The Anaconda' Danson would have probably eaten the canine thief and thus claimed another, albeit indirect, ten-pie haul).

Controversy was enthusiastically courted in later years when outside pies were supplied to the event, thus breaking Wigan's monopoly; this does

matter in these parts, since Wigan residents are known universally as 'pie-eaters'. The etymology is supposedly derived form the 1926 General Strike, when acute financial hardship necessitated Wigan miners to return to work and were thus deemed to have eaten 'humble pie'.

A world record was set in 2005 when the aforementioned Anthony 'The Anaconda' Danson scoffed seven pies in 3 minutes; since event rules decree that pies must conform to a minimum diameter of 12cm and a depth of 3.5cm, this means he may well have been a real anaconda – not sure if the judges checked that.

The event remains familiar with controversy, as the 2009 competition endured allegations of gravy-rigging when cough syrup was allegedly added to the pies to maximise speedy consumption and emollient throaty slip-down. More recent events have included stringent officialdom, and anyone turning up with a carrier bag containing a meat pie and several bottles of cough syrup will be either banned from the Pie Eating Championship, or the worst ever contestant on *Ready Steady Cook*.

Forty-two-year-old Neil Collier required a mere 23.9 seconds to obtain the world record in 2010 – other competitors had barely progressed through their crust to reach the meat when the judges indicated

they had a winner. There then followed a tension-raising wait while 'sweepers' ensured no more than a legally permitted regulatory one ounce of crumbs had been shed. After the crumbs were declared legal, the crowd cheered – with the occasional boo, given that he was from Bolton. Apparently this is a very bad thing.

A healthy number of competitors (yes, I'm aware that phrase is fraught with porous irony) continue to enter the contest each year, although we still await the ultimate competition – and if Sky are prepared to put up the money, surely we can see the Big One: John Prescott v Eric Pickles. That would settle the big question once and for all: Who ate all the pies?

Pooh Sticks
WORLD CHAMPIONSHIP

uestion: How many sports have produced a reigning world champion aged under ten? No, I can't think of another one either. Thus, in claiming the 2011 annual Pooh Sticks World Championship ahead of nearly 500 other competitors, nine-year-old Saffron Sollitt from Wallingford probably became the youngest ever sporting world champion. She told waiting TV camera crews, 'I chose the area where the river was running faster.' Can't argue with that. 'And I think choosing a nicely coloured stick helped.' (Probably can argue with that.)

When I first attended this event, the winter weather was so mercilessly cold that I recall stepping over a dead bird on the riverbank, speculating that it had probably died from hypothermia; I think it was a penguin. It was one of those pitilessly cold days when you keep imagining there must be an extra higher button on your coat, inducing constant checking to discover that the jacket really is already snugly buttoned all the way to the very top, and yet still an icy wind pervades with a penetrative capacity to howl through your entire fibrous being.

This is probably why I am now returning in late March, whereas the event was previously held in December. However, the additional light and minuscule extra warmth available from the calendar switch is offset by other difficulties for the Pooh Sticks purist to endure: namely the sheer popularity of the event. Having parked the car in the nearest available remaining spot to the contest (which means neighbouring Berkshire), it's a long walk to the bridge at Day's Lock nestled between Long Wittenham and Dorchester-on-Thames in Oxfordshire. Be warned, this is one busy event masquerading as the unofficial annual outing for Middle England.

Adults, as well as children, loudly cheer on their sticks – believing they respond to encouragement. Then again, with a 6ft anthropomorphic tiger and bear walking around taking pictures on their phones, it's probably not the place to lecture children with reality lessons.

The sport itself isn't necessarily that enthralling. Because there are so many players, the event becomes extremely samey, with line after line of contestants dropping colour-coded sticks into the onrushing River Thames. There are undoubtable advantages to be obtained by selecting the optimum angles, but ultimately the size of the field, and flow of the river, renders the winner crowned by luck rather than technique.

Competitors stand at the side of the bridge with arms extended, then lower them to meet the level of the shortest person (otherwise diminutive participants would have an advantage, given their stick would hit flowing water first). The starter is meticulous about another technique of reaching the water before your opponent's sticks – namely throwing them – and insists on a steady drop after, 'Ready . . . Steady . . . Go'; his final syllable has only just decayed into the spring Oxfordshire air, as the first stick hits the water. Disqualifications duly occur, with several sticks dropped prematurely albeit motivated by enthusiasm rather than mendacity. Players immediately sprint across the bridge to await the reappearance of their stick – which means it's not a good time to be using the bridge as a pedestrian.

The event is rightly popular, and features lots of young children shouting 'poo' – but in a good way.

Pram Racing

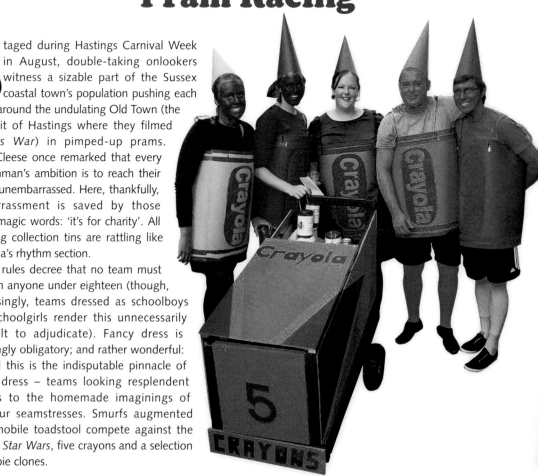

Staged during Hastings Carnival Week in August, double-taking onlookers witness a sizable part of the Sussex coastal town's population pushing each other around the undulating Old Town (the nice bit of Hastings where they filmed *Foyle's War*) in pimped-up prams. John Cleese once remarked that every Englishman's ambition is to reach their grave unembarrassed. Here, thankfully, embarrassment is saved by those three magic words: 'it's for charity'. All evening collection tins are rattling like Santana's rhythm section.

The rules decree that no team must contain anyone under eighteen (though, confusingly, teams dressed as schoolboys and schoolgirls render this unnecessarily difficult to adjudicate). Fancy dress is seemingly obligatory; and rather wonderful: indeed this is the indisputable pinnacle of fancy dress – teams looking resplendent thanks to the homemade imaginings of amateur seamstresses. Smurfs augmented with mobile toadstool compete against the cast of *Star Wars*, five crayons and a selection of Barbie clones.

Prams cannot surpass a generous 8ft by 5ft dimension – which would certainly be indicative of a preposterously big baby. The pram racing circuit starts and ends at the Cutter public house, with teams obligated to obtain signature proof that they visited all the prescribed pubs on the route, though this equates to an incredible cumulative nineteen pubs to visit! Not that anyone retains the ability to count once they've visited nineteen pubs in the same evening. And like most athletes, participants sensibly warm up before the race by downing numerous tinnies.

Fortunately the potentially lethal mix of alcohol and no brakes rarely presents a danger, given the sheer number of participants regularly blocking the circuit, aided and abetted in their speed-reduction techniques by a surging crowd of spectators regularly spilling out onto the route.

107

Expressing a refreshingly lackadaisical approach to competitive team sport regulations, the rules refuse to limit team size. Teams of radically fluctuating numbers push their colourful prams with the drunkest member having a sleep-it-off lie down inside the pram.

The opening race exclusively attracts a group of boy racers – mainly because it's a race for boys aged under fourteen. The children's races feature noticeably more mature conduct than the adult race. Although mainly a wonderfully good-humoured charity event, one of the more competitive teams treated spectators to an acrimonious bust-up: one pram-pusher's apoplectic anger ensured he petulantly hurled his fancy dress props onto the Hastings tarmac; thankfully he was the only competitor throwing his toys out of the pram.

Creative, colourful fun supporting good causes – one of the best things it's possible to see in August.

Real Tennis

To be fair to Eton and their supposed privileges, instead of complaining when someone built a garage extension protruding straight onto their tennis court, and abandoning the sport in a huff, they merely adapted the rules and carried on playing tennis around the newly built obstacle. That being the only likely explanation as to how Real Tennis courts ended up with an invasive wall ('tambour') and angled roof inside them.

And what's not to like about a sport that is even hubristic in its very name? 'Real' Tennis implies that it is the one true racquet sport, not this phoney imposter, Lawn Tennis. No, because Real Tennis is the bona fide, genuine article.

Of course, evidence for this actually being the undisputed true 'real' tennis is probably best completely ignored, as there isn't any – especially since there are only 47 real tennis courts existing on the planet. Luckily, over half of these are in Britain. Which means – take note, world – we're rather good at it. Yes, yes – USA, Switzerland, Spain and Eastern European countries with freakishly tall robotic serving machines are all quite good at fake tennis, but Britain dominates Real Tennis. Ideally, we should demolish Wimbledon's Centre Court, and replace it with a complex of Real Tennis courts, where Britons can go on to meet fellow Britons in rounds 2, 3, 4, 5 and the final (although, annoyingly, an Australian has got rather good at the sport in recent years – Robert Fahey has dominated the bi-annual world championship of late – but only for the last twenty years (!)).

Real Tennis is a wonderfully eccentric sport played on a bizarre walled court with sloping roofs, yet is sufficiently historical to be namechecked by Shakespeare in *Henry V*. Real Tennis also claims to have the longest continuous line of world champions in any sport. Its image is certainly on the pampered side of posh, with Henry VIII building a designated court at Hampton Court, while shameless royal sycophants Oxford and Cambridge Universities followed suit. Perhaps surprisingly, the North also features on the sport's radar – with Jesmond and Salford both possessing functioning courts. Eccentrically, a picture of a unicorn (or monarch – each court differs) is situated in one corner; known as the 'grille', striking it wins the point, as does hitting the 'dedans' (a netted area behind the server).

Real Tennis players don't do tie-breaks, so whoever reaches six games first captures the set, regardless of whether it's 6–5. The sport has another clever innovation that Lawn Tennis has surprisingly not yet imitated: a shallow sloping channel runs beneath the central net conveniently collecting balls in a bucket – dispensing with the need for ball boys.

By way of gauging the game's actual universal appeal, it is worth noting that there are only two current manufacturers of Real Tennis racquets in the world: one in Cambridge and the other in Denver, Colorado: which means casual converts are unlikely to discover a racquet in TK Maxx's sale. Fitting with the game's eccentric image is the wool-covered ball, which is predominantly manufactured from cork – similar to a cricket ball; it is a much harder ball than those usually associated with racquet sports.

Royal Shrovetide Football

There's a vaguely intimidating odour of alcohol on the breath among some participants – always concerning in a morning. A profusion of old-style rugby shirts is also in evidence – none of these modern, beer-belly-emphasising, skin-tight designs, thank you. Then the numbers swell, with more and more people arriving. Estimates are put at between 3,500 and 5,000, all standing in a car park, at lunchtime on a work day, to compete in one of Britain's most eccentric and historical football matches.

Royal Shrovetide Football occurs in the quaint and otherwise inconspicuous Derbyshire town of Ashbourne on Shrove Tuesday and Ash Wednesday – a custom that's divaricated the town for several centuries. Teams of locals known as Up'ards and Down'ards split the town into the two halves, both pursuing goals spaced 3 miles apart.

This is mad. Madder than a madman who's been asked to leave a mad hatter's tea party for being unnecessarily mad. And just when observance has crystallised into realisation that this whole game couldn't become any madder, the scrimmaging players then move from the streets to participate in the river. I think that's worth typing again: the players then move into the river.

Enthusiastically piling into the freezing muddy murk of the River Henmore, countless players wade into a mass aquatic fight. This has now become the sort of thing that *It's A Knockout* would reject for being too silly.

I once attended a football game (as in conventional river-free soccer) between Runcorn and Boston United, which ended with a mass brawl – perhaps the only time when the ball has been left rejected and neglected while twenty-two players preferred to pile into each other with fist-swinging alacrity. Not even one lone player had the foresight or desire to dribble the recently abandoned ball unopposed towards the opponents' unguarded vacant goal. And there are several occasions in this match where you suspect something similar has happened as the ball cannot be spotted for great swathes of time – mainly because it's in the middle of a vast scrum (known as 'the hug'). Then, after 10 minutes a rare glimpse of ball, and then it disappears again for another 20 minutes. Most ball games don't really work as spectator sports if the spectators only see the ball twice in several hours, and only occasional coruscating glimpses occur as a gigantic scrum moves the ball slowly forward like a vast human centipede.

Emerging from the river, all humanity is completely covered in mud – resembling in both looks and

personality, how mankind must have appeared when it first emerged from the primordial soup. There is certainly a paucity of rules in this sport. And yet there is also identifiable warmth between players, with concern for each other and their historic custom. But the absence of rules doesn't lead to an absence of authority. The result of a recent game was not announced until the next day, following a swiftly convened judicial review that declared a winning 'goal' should be negated after interviewing witnesses established the ball was 'goaled' after the permitted 10 p.m. deadline. The Down'ards may have thrown the rule book out of the window, but the Up'ards, sensing foul play, ensured they threw the rule book straight back through the same window.

Whether you're a loyal Up'ard or Down'ard pivots on which side of the river you were born. This is always likely to be slightly arbitrary, but I can foresee the Up'ards forming a domineering advantage as the years progress – given Up'ard's territory is the location of the town's new maternity hospital!!

Loyalties, understandably, can be divided in a close-knit community. Dougie Sowter switched sides mid-game in 1972 and ran towards his own goal to score. He justified this as a request of his mother, a lone Up'ard in a family of Down'ards, but it is reported he has consequently been blanked by two aunties ever since.

Following a civilised parade and a formal luncheon, a dignitary commences the game at 2 p.m. by throwing the ball from a brick plinth in the town's Shaw Croft car park. Prince Charles was the 'turner-upper' (the official term) in 2003. Another Prince of Wales, soon to become Edward VIII, had earlier performed the same duty in 1928.

The 2010's game turn-up honours were bestowed upon John Harrison in recognition of over 20 years of ball making. At one stage in that year's game a substantial hole opened up in the Up'ards' defence – this time of the completely literal variety – when a forgotten well was suddenly exposed. As if the alarm bells weren't already ringing for the Down'ards, a fire engine turned up and parked on top of it to cover the hazard from players and spectators.

2011 saw the first game for over 75 years to feature four goals, with the ball goaled in each of the 3-mile-apart targets over the two days. Simon Fisher equalised for the Up'ards just minutes before the enforced 10 p.m. close of play, thus forcing the Down'ards to return their champagne to the fridge.

Climbing skills are also shown to be apparent, as is the necessity not to park anywhere in Ashbourne during the game. In a recent game a milk float was ruined when players crushed it while scrambling over it to reach the ball – still, no point in crying over spilt milk.

Additional local colour is added to the event by players' partners. Present throughout, and adorned in meretricious luminous pink tops, are a group of perennially smiling effervescent ladies, tops emblazoned with the word 'SWAGS' which, upon questioning, apparently stands for 'Shrovetide Wives And Girlfriends'; presumably an earlier planning stage rejected Shrovetide Lovers And Girlfriends. (I'll wait.)

Oh, and in case you're wondering: the royal prefix originates from Edward VIII unwisely participating; he gained a bloody nose, rendering him one of the least injured participants in the game's history.

Scrabble

BRITISH CHAMPIONSHIP

There is a place in Wales that has a ridiculously long name – you probably know the village I'm referring to, but have no recollection what it's called – mainly because it has over 50 letters in its name. However, the Welsh are formidable at Scrabble, as they can make creative high-scoring use of all those 'L', 'W' and 'Y' tiles, coveted by the Welsh, yet feared and rejected by the English tiler.

My Scrabble opponent might as well be playing in Welsh, the sense that I'm able to attribute to the word she plays. I play 'GETA' followed by 'LIFE'. A

116

spectator laughs. My opponent doesn't. But she does feel sufficiently moved to do one thing: thrash me.

Scrabble once had an image problem, but it's now moved out of the parlour (just as well, as seemingly the only people in Britain still in possession of parlours tend to work in either the funeral or massage industries) and into hotel function rooms. This is the competitive environment where the British Championships are held. After a contemplative 2 minutes, she leans forward purposefully and lays down seven tiles. For those not au fait with Scrabble, this is Bingo. I know, it's got confusing. A bingo (noun) is the act of bingoing (verb), wherein a Scrabble player plays their entire seven-tile hand in one play, thus earning an additional 50-point bonus. She takes a dispiritingly short amount of time to total '112 points', due to various triple letter, double word and quadruple vowel scores (I suspect she exploited my Scrabble naivety by merely making one of those up – come on, who's heard of 'double word score'?).

Almost every word played in modern day competitive Scrabble is virtually unrecognisable to the average English speaker. Hence becoming a contemporary Scrabble champion necessitates learning endless vocab lists like an overseas student cramming for an English exam. Only most of these words would rarely be deployed in natural conversation during a person's lifetime, the board being scattered with a proliferation of technical medical terms and the name of an extinct South American shrew. Bizarrely, offensive swear words are permitted, though playing the seven-letter word 'Cameron' isn't. Disappointingly, players are unable to provide definitions of the words they've learned, preferring not to allocate vital brain capacity to storing the word's meaning. Hence lists rather than dictionaries are studied, and the industry standard list is the annually reviewed *Collins Scrabble Word List*.

The 2011 version added words such as 'twiglet' (yeah, the crispy snack) and, controversially, 'innit'. The Collins list is studied for hours by committed players. Innit. And research pays off. At a tournament in Manchester in 1982, an astonishing 380 points were claimed for laying down 'caziques'; this play earned Kurdish contestant Karl Khoshnaw a considerable prize – he actually succeeded in earning more money for laying down seven tiles than a self-employed builder. Caziques are ancient Inca princesses; Khoshnaw would have been unlikely to have known that. But definitions are not required to win Scrabble tournaments – that's the reality of the modern game, and it's necessary to conform to that mindset for a fun night out on the tiles.

Scrabble was devised in the 1930s by American architect Alfred Butts. Finding himself unemployed in the Depression, Butts invented a Scrabble prototype that he initially titled Lexico. He then painstakingly checked newspapers to ascertain the frequency with which letters reoccurred in articles, and allocated a scoring value to each letter according to its rarity.

The British Championships have been contested annually since June 1971 when it was inaugurated by author and broadcaster Gyles Brandreth bringing together 100 Scrabble contestants. Nowadays seeded entrants have to overcome regional qualifying tournaments, in order to progress to a fourteen-game semi-final weekend, where the two highest achieving players progress to the grand final in London. The tournament spans a wide range of ages (fifteen-year-old Allan Saldanha winning in 1993) and genders, with transsexual Mikki Nicholson holding aloft the 2010 trophy while resplendent in a pink wig and fuchsia PVC dress. Nicholson played 'inficete' (meaning 'unfunny') to beat Mark Nyman who had previously bagged the British Championship on no less than four occasions, topping this by being crowned Britain's only Scrabble World Champion. Nyman became world champion in 1993, overcoming his Canadian opponent Joel Wapnick with a remarkable 3–2 turnaround in the final, after being 1–2 down and then trailing by 174 points in a game he eventually won. However, Lady Luck was evidently detained in traffic when the same pair contested the world championship final six years later – the former inhabitant of *Countdown's* Dictionary Corner lost the decider by a wafer-thin 402 to 403 points margin. But that's the luck of the tile bag. Innit.

Shin Kicking
CHAMPIONSHIPS

In the same way that seaside towns are dominated by the ceaseless sound of seagulls, the identifiable Cotswolds sound is the polite chinking of china cups and the metallic clatter of butter knife against scone plate. So it's odd to the point of unnerving to discover this defining Cotswold sound is temporarily replaced once a year with cries of, 'go on, kick him!' revealing mankind's primitive instinct to have only received a shallow coating of civilisation.

'Break a leg,' shouts a corpulent man, thoroughly aware he's not in a theatre.

In the otherwise charmingly civilised Cotswold conurbation of Chipping Campden, civilisation is pulled back for a couple of hours on a Friday in June each year as several grown men repeatedly make use of temporarily suspended social restraint to kick each other as hard as they possibly can on the shins. There are undoubtedly better things to do in the Cotswolds than this, and most of the alternatives involve tea shops. However, while the aloof Olympics continually

discard Shin Kicking as a bona fide sport, perspicacious sports fans, knowledgeable of the games' origins, will inform you that the Olympics started here. That's right. The Cotswolds. Evidence? OK, I have some. Records show that Robert Dover opened the 'Olimpicks' in 1612, and they've been happening on Dover's Hill above Chipping Campden ever since. So, that's just under 400 years before Athens resurrected the Modern Olympics; hmm, close. And Robert Drover (and Shropshire's Much Wenlock) provided better prizes; in the original Isthmian Games (*c.* 500 BC), victorious Greek athletes received a celery hat (!) and 100 drachma (probably loaned from the EU).

People flock to the Cotswolds each year to attend the Olimpicks, a spectacular array of seventeenth-century heraldry and games, of which the star attraction is undoubtedly Shin Kicking. That said, Shin Kicking would be a poor day out in isolation. What paying spectators get is: firstly, two blokes dressed like eighteenth-century farmers kicking each other on the shins while clutching each other's shoulders. Secondly . . . OK, there is no 'secondly' – the 'firstly' entirely covers the sport.

Surprisingly, a large crowd has assembled to watch shins being kicked. A brief departure from ennui-inducing predictability occurs when one competitor runs away – a sensible rather than cowardly act in my book, but apparently he had already lost. People applaud, the PA man does his best to raise enthusiasm and the rep from Britain's largest shin pad supplier

has picked an incredibly unfortunate week to be on holiday. Having said that, I intend to attend next year – manning my 'Get your shin pads here' stall, as currently competitors prefer the home-made approach of tying supplied straw around their legs.

There is also inherent danger in winning this event as – not unlike Ireland naively winning the Eurovision Song Contest for several consecutive years, seemingly unaware that the winner had to keep hosting it – whoever wins the Shin Kicking Championship is forced to return next year and be kicked again. Yes, it is better than a kick in the head – but only by about a 4 or 5ft margin.

Snail Racing
WORLD CHAMPIONSHIP

On your marks, get set, go! Go! GO! And we'll be back in an hour to see if anyone's moved. Welcome to the Snail Racing World Championship, held each July in a cricket field in Congham, Norfolk. Snails wear a numbered sticker, pressed like a price label onto their shells, which makes them look like they've escaped from an aisle in a French supermarket.

If polo possesses the record for the largest officially designated playing area in sport, then this could be a contender for the smallest. This is certainly not a marathon – though it's unquestionably not a sprint, either. Tempting lettuce reclines on the outer edge of the circle, beckoning enticingly to the shelled competitors. It's a slimy business, snail racing, as is proven by the glistening trails marking the lanes taken by the competitors as they slither and slide towards the lettuce line.

Snails race outwards from the centre of a circular table; Sidney the Snail eventually emerging victorious in the 2010 contest, taking a mere 3 minutes 41 seconds (fast – relatively – but incomparable to world record holder Archie the Snail who took a dismissively short 2 minutes 13 seconds to complete the course and reach lettuce glory at the 1995 event).

However, not all snails race towards the lettuce line. Some opt to replicate Wayne Rooney's performance at the 2010 World Cup and refuse to leave the centre circle throughout the tournament. 2011's race was run at a slow pace (probably shouldn't have been surprised by that), and the lettuce line crossed just as the descending sun opted to depart Norfolk for another day, temporarily illuminating the field in mellow sinking light.

Beating molluscs from as far away as Japan, ironically named local entrant Zoomer, picked up from a King's Lynn garden, required just under 3 and a half minutes to claim the 2011 world championship title. An awards ceremony concludes the race, where Zoomer – unnoticeably refulgent in victory – receives his prize: more lettuce.

Stilton Cheese Rolling
WORLD CHAMPIONSHIP

I've had this dream before – it must be the cheese. A witty dwarf with a microphone gently chips away at the tolerance of four burly bearded men now noticeably regretting

wearing pink tutus, while a woman dressed as Snow White attempts to roll an impractically large Stilton cheese through a town centre street closed to traffic. Although possible to encounter eccentricity fatigue when exposed to multiple events featured in this book, the core weirdness of this event remains undiluted by comparison.

Teams comprising four players race against others while attempting to roll Stilton like a recently dislodged tyre along the mainly even surface of the main street in Stilton, Cambridgeshire. A profusion of fancy dress costumes ensures the event flowers with colour, and provides a reassurance that matters are not supposed to be taken too seriously. Not that the event needs to get any weirder or more spurious, but it's accurate to report that Stilton cheese was historically sold rather than made in Stilton. Oh well. But that could be changing, with Stilton expected to be granted a production licence.

Although undeniably related in shared cheese rolling eccentricity, Stilton rolling differs considerably from the collective madness of its counterpart at Cooper's Hill, Gloucestershire, by being a considerably more sensible, although younger, sibling. A crucial difference is that the smart people of Stilton have decided to roll their cheeses on a sensibly flat and predominately tarmac-covered surface. Thus the

St John Ambulance turnout is immeasurably smaller, yet unequally active.

Stilton provides a large-scale old-fashioned village fête each May Day, with numerous family-friendly events from guess the weight of the cake in the morning to an *X Factor*-style contest in the evening. There's certainly a pleasing atmosphere, celebrating an unflinching Britishness personified by seeing a vicar dunk a homemade scone while complimenting a lady on her pert chrysanthemums (definitely not a euphemism). Elgar's music begins to saturate my brain.

No one seems sure when and how Stilton Rolling began, though this didn't preclude organisers from billing the 2009 event as their fiftieth anniversary. This rough dating is redeemable, given that the tradition probably started once the Great North Road (or to deploy its less descriptive title: the A1) bypassed Stilton around this time, and the town's hostelries also found themselves suddenly bypassed by trade.

Judges ensure each team member participates in the roll. Adopting a knock-out structure, two teams eventually meet in the final with a Stilton and beer for the winning men's team, and Stilton and white wine for the victorious ladies (the prizes presumably prescribed by Al Murray). Celebrities have been spotted at the event: charismatic actors Warwick Davis and Robbie Coltrane – the latter probably no stranger to large portions of delicious British cheese – were recently observed supporting this hugely enjoyable event.

Stone Skimming
WORLD CHAMPIONSHIPS

ere's the first rule of Stone Skimming Club: no one can attend the event for more than 10 minutes without making a reference to the Dam Busters. In truth, this is not technically correct as one person did manage to attend the whole world championship in 2010 without making such a reference, but it later transpired that he was German.

The world championship is decided by who skims the stone the furthest – although that description merely skims the surface. Distance, some would-be entrants are surprised to learn, rather than the number of skims, is the currency that buys you the world championship. This is contested by some, who would prefer to see multiple skimmers rewarded, perhaps signposting a future rival breakaway world

championship akin to the imbroglios in boxing, chess and darts which led to competing dual federations both singularly claiming that they're THE true world championship.

In the meantime, the governing world centre of the sport is situated in the Inner Hebrides. The championships are well organised, with various entertainments creating a sense of occasion in this charmingly remote part of the UK, with an ebullient folk punk band providing music that struggles to be audible against a relentless northern wind. That wind is blowing today, and local inhabitants tell of being fourteen years old when they first recollected a day without the otherwise ceaseless wind, and once it stopped blowing everyone consequently fell over.

But people are on their feet today, even if they are perpetually angled at a counteracting 20 degrees. The rules of international stone skimming decree that a stone must skim the surface on a minimum of three occasions; only then is the distance measured. Hence, if your stone travels so far after launching that it circles the globe to hit you in the back of the neck after its return via the North Sea from circumnavigating the planet, but it only bounced twice, then it doesn't count and will be beaten by a stone that's struggled to travel a whole metre after its legal triple skim.

Some players possess the necessary wrist strength and dexterity through training exercises (I'll leave a space now for you to add your own teenage boy joke)

and are natural skimmers. Others try hard, but only manage to skim the surface of success (see what I did there?). Others are less Dam Busters, more U-Boat, and their efforts repeatedly drop, er, well, like a stone.

The championships occur in September on Easdale Island (near Oban) – the smallest of all the permanently inhabited Inner Hebridean islands. In the 2010 Championships, runner-up Paul Crabtree hit the back harbour wall (over 60 metres), meaning that winner Dougie Isaacs eventually had to accomplish the feat twice. Founded in 1983 (though it lay dormant again until the mid-1990s), the event provides both individual and team world champions. The traditional British stranglehold on the event was recently unlocked by a German winning the Women's World Championship.

Tar Barrels

ttery St Mary in Devon extols itself as Britain's most pyromaniac town by staging the annual Tar Barrels event each 5 November. Spectators are rarely disappointed as this is one sporting contest that regularly catches fire (as well as the participants, some members of the crowd and anything on the route unwisely made of flammable materials). The route is filled with thick acrid smoke and burning bitumen, rendering spectators gasping for clean air to purify their lungs. There's more smoke than the average back entrance to an office building. Or school toilet. And yet it's wonderful to behold.

Contestants wear something akin to a pair of oversized oven mittens – these are designed from ragged sack cloth for practicality rather than aesthetics, and are unlikely to be found in Debenhams in a range endorsed by Marco Pierre White. It is genuinely terrifying – seriously strong people holding 20kg barrels aloft and performing balancing curlicues at speed would be reasonably scary – but did I mention they're on fire? Large orange flames dart like dragons' tongues out of transported barrels' mouths. One contestant's bulging portliness proves to be no restrainer of speed.

On first seeing the tar barrel spectacle, the initial instinct is to be frightened, denounce it as 'crazy' and phone the authorities. After watching it for several minutes, you still feel frightened, denounce it as crazy and want to dial 999. And yet, there's something undeniably marvellous and captivating about it – they're not technically racing, it's more of a community parade – yet as a spectacle it is hypnotically compelling, with senses of smell, sight, sound and danger all aroused to the maximum. It's

also one of the few sports where you retain the uncomfortable impression that neither competitors nor organisers are fully content admitting spectators – an area where other sports have surely been going wrong, with all their cheap pandering to commercial revenue streams, needy paying spectators and broadcasting rights diluting their sport's purity.

An organising official, politeness justifiably worn down by recalcitrant members of the public complaining about barrels on fire at a barrels on fire event billed as Tar Barrels On Fire (I know), signed off the event's website with, 'If after all this you still decide to attend make sure you check our tag on safety,' before concluding 'and remember you are not there for our benefit,' which is a reassuringly refreshing approach towards spectators.

This is the ultimate day out for all pyromaniacs, fire starters and that scary bloke from The Prodigy. Behaviour that in any other location on any other day would see you back in borstal, is celebrated by a huge Guy Fawkes crowd. The date provides a clue to the event's origins, as many consider this centuries-old tradition commenced in about 1605 – the date of Fawkes' thwarted London terrorist attack.

Sharing similarly opaque origins with several other eccentric British pastimes, there are counter anecdotes hypothesising its genesis. Some promulgate that Devonians lit tar barrels to warn of invading Spaniards, a tactic which would have probably worked: spotting through ship's binoculars numerous locals running around carrying enormous barrels on fire would certainly put me off coming ashore.

Another proposed theory is that tar barrels were a primitive fumigation ritual – although setting one's house on fire would certainly address that troubling earwig problem, albeit one later evaluated as a somewhat pyrrhic success when the insurance people made contact. However, a sizable majority infer that it commenced as a Guy Fawkes tradition, and certainly 1605 is generally claimed as a starting date.

Tiddlywinks

A true British sport, 'Tiddledy-Winks' was invented in 1888 by London shop owner Joseph Assheton Fincher. The world's first Tiddlywinks club (the superfluous 'ed' had long since been filed off by 1954) was inaugurated at Cambridge University, and it is to the light blue Fenland seat of learning that players return each year to wink their tiddlys (or should that be the other way around?). By 1958 *The Times* had printed the association's rules for a world championship.

Polite panel parlour game *Call My Bluff* ran for several series, but would have struggled to find sufficient bizarre words for a single episode were it not for the anomalous neology mined from the nation's eccentric sports. Tiddlywinks contributed to our isle's enriched vocabulary by coining the word 'squop', when an opponent's tiddlywink is covered by another counter. A 'boondock' is a liberated, freed squop, while a 'penhaligon' is a potted wink from the base line (an approximate tiddlywinks version of a hole-in-one). Meanwhile, a 'scrounge' is a shot rebounding off the cup. A 'squidger' is the circular disc players use to flick their winks. Surprisingly, players can use their own squidgers, with liberal rules governing size and construction materials. Top players carry a considerable number of squidgers, sometimes selecting different ones for assorted shots like a (far more portable and less likely to block up the hall) bag of golf clubs. Uncovered winks can legitimately be described as 'unsquopped'. Indeed, in games where potted winks are equal, unstoppable unsquopped winks then determine the victor.

There's even a national English tiddlywinks association: known as ETwA. They produce a (surprisingly good) magazine wholly devoted to tiddlywinks, and it's surely only a matter of time before it fulfils its inevitable destiny of being featured

on *Have I Got News For You*. Especially since the title is: *Winking World*.

Games are usually composed of two players per side, and intercontinental challenges have occurred. An Oxford University team arrived in the USA in 1963, and proceeded to impose several defeats on them, in retaliation for their hosts wasting all that tea in a minor skirmish in 1766. The match at Harvard featured cheerleaders, but the Brits defeated 23 consecutive US teams! *Life* magazine was forced to concede, 'The best tiddlywinks player in America appears to be only slightly better than the worst in England.'

Providing intriguing continuity, some of those 1963 American players' offsprings are now keen Tiddlywinks exponents themselves – perhaps vowing revenge for their fathers' humiliations (surely that's a movie pitch?). Indeed, after decades of British dominance the current World Singles Champion is (*cough, lowers voice*) an American. Reports are also reaching these shores of squidgers being purposefully pressed in Eastern Europe and Australia. So Britain's dominant world status is not unsquoppable.

Tiddlywinks offers considerable fun, and is pleasingly inclusive: it's one of the cheapest games in existence, can be played anywhere there's a table, and all ages from small children to centenarians can easily participate. Plus Britain's dominated the sport for 125 years!

Tin Bath

W O R L D   C H A M P I O N S H I P S

Firstly, a rather poorly concealed clue in the official rules as to competitors' chances of success: 'the winner will be the first to finish the course or the one covering the most distance' i.e. rather ominously, it's unlikely that anyone will finish the course without sinking. 'Sinking' appears several times in the official rules. An event organiser revealed to the *IOM Courier*, 'We had 50 men in 2010 and only 12 finishers. The ladies are more stable. It must be something to do with their hair.' Controversial.

Alarming talk of sinking and drowning may have already alerted you to the fact this is a water-based discipline. This is not dry land tin bath racing, a

ever since. At times the sport resembles aquatic dodgems, with illicit bumper car clangs competing against seagull shrills.

Alongside separate men's and women's races, the event also attracts several sailors, salted with experience from regular participation, who compete in the veterans' race. In the women's race, Erika Cowen won the title for an incredible thirteenth time in 2010; other competitors did enter the women's race during those thirteen years – I checked! But Erika's reign was usurped in 2011 when she was beaten into second place by her own daughter Greta. However, a recent men's race was tethered to controversy – with illegal cable ties. Described by *IOM Today* as 'surreptitious enhancements', an organiser informed the local paper: 'scrutineers

fictional sport seemingly popularised by *Last of the Summer Wine* where three old blokes wander aimlessly around the country pointlessly crashing things in over 300 episodes (sorry, that's *Top Gear*).

No, the true Tin Bath Racing World Championship occurs in water – water of the murky, salty and much deeper-than-putting-your-feet-on-the-bottom depth in the Middle Harbour of Castletown, Isle of Man. Far less of an air and sound pollutant than the Isle's other famous race, the TT, the Tin Bath Racing World Championship started in 1971 (two competitors in the fortieth anniversary race had paddled in all 40 races) and has attracted considerable spectator numbers

discovered 5 or 6 tin baths had employed cable ties – a well known illegal enhancement – to secure their floats.' Naughty.

Someone who probably should have used surreptitious floating enhancements was TV's Ben Fogle, who gamely participated in the event, only to sink three times in a few minutes – a noble embarrassment unkindly captured for posterity on YouTube.

The contest's origins are appropriately eccentric. Monied industrialist Henry Kremer, having purchased a holiday retreat on the island, offered a £50,000 prize in 1959 to anyone possessing man-powered flight capability; a boast they would have to demonstrate by flying a mile from Castletown harbour in full view of his house – which would have been unfortunate for anyone accomplishing this challenge when he was out. Since the only mammals capable of flight are bats – and the rules almost certainly prevented bats from entering – this was a relatively safe, if incomprehensibly daft, wager. That was until 1977 when a hang-glider operative claimed the prize: the successful craft is currently displayed in

Washington's Smithsonian Museum. Until the unlikely claiming of the prize, numerous Bognor Birdman-type eccentrics routinely donned a traffic cone on their head and then fearlessly pedalled a bike off the harbour wall. Such behaviour was clearly more beneficial to local charities than the A&E department at Douglas Hospital. The tin baths were initially used as improvised rescue vehicles, and in 1971 it was decided to formalise the races, given that many tin baths had previously raced each other to be first on the scene to rescue failed flyers.

It's a quirky and deceptively difficult event, celebrating the Isle of Man's nautical tradition in front of annual crowds of over 4,000, while raising considerable sums for charity. The Isle of Man has created a rather wonderful, colourful addition to the noble canon of British eccentric sports. Long may it stay afloat.

Toad in the Hole

A s (hopefully) every dinner party host knows, making Toad in the Hole doesn't involve frantically searching Waitrose's shelves for toads. Likewise no actual buffaloes feature in buffalo mozzarella, and no amphibians are harmed in the annual Toad in the Hole World Championship. Although actual holes are involved.

While devoid of amphibians throughout, the toads in this context are small metallic disks that are lobbed into a hole in a table. The table has a drawer which opens to reveal the number of toads in the hole, hence the name. An announcer declares the start of one match by orating, 'Each player will in turn toss off four toads' (oh, grow up). Not intentional comedy, but it does raise sniggers. Toads are then hurled towards, what appear to the spectator non-conversant with the sport, as impractically small holes – most land noisily on the table, remaining stubbornly above ground. Soon I suspect the targeted holes are smaller than the toads. Eventually a more experienced player succeeds in creating the first subterranean toads. He looks pleased, yet simultaneously rueful that he didn't accomplish more – perhaps he was expecting to receive a bagged goldfish.

Two teams, comprising four players, contest each game. Each player throws four toads when visiting

the table, with teams competing to be the first side to reach zero by counting down from 31 points. Two points are awarded each time a toad is sunk into a hole, and a single point is collected for any toad that remains on the table-top. However, should a player sink a toad with all four throws in the same visit to the table (a rare if not impossible occurrence), then they automatically win the game outright.

The world championship is conducted in Lewes, East Sussex: a town that's presumably intent on establishing itself as the Wembley of eccentric sports, given the proliferation of richly idiosyncratic games (Dwile Flonking, Pea Throwing . . . OK that's it) here.

Both the Toad in the Hole European Masters and the World Championships are decided, unsurprisingly, in Lewes too – it's basically contested by forty people, all from Lewes, but hey – that's in Europe and the World, right?

And, like Aunt Sally in Oxfordshire, a national debt of gratitude is owed to the worthy people of Sussex for enthusiastically conserving this historic sport and keeping it off the extinction register. It's an enjoyable game, offering easy participation and social interaction for all ages. And no toads are hurt in the making.

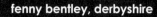

Toe Wrestling

WORLD CHAMPIONSHIP

Spreading fun, frivolity and fungal infection since 1970, the World Toe Wrestling Championship sees the sport's best exponents lock toes in an annual contest of determined wrestling and appalling puns. Dominating both categories are the sport's hottest three tickets: Paul Beech known as The Toeminator, Nasty Nash and . . . ahem . . . all the way from Milan it's The Itatoelian Stallion – a pun so bad it can probably cause superficial damage to buildings.

Held at the Royal Oak pub in Wetton since inception, the event relocated in 2003 to the Bentley Brook Inn in the wonderfully named village of Fenny Bentley near Ashbourne in Derbyshire. The sport was initiated by local George Burgess in a reasonable fit of patriotism: he wished to invent a sport that would provide a British world champion. Hence Toe Wrestling was conceived – a plan that was partially successful, given the inaugural world championship was won

by the only non-UK dweller present: a Canadian. Recognising a setback when they saw one, the event was then immediately mothballed for several years (although that could have been to hide the stinky foot odour).

Nowadays the contest rigorously complies with the rules of the world famous World Toe Wrestling Organisation (no, me neither), with two competitors locking big toes and commencing to wrestle upon the referee's shout, 'toes away!' Continuing the sport's propensity for punning, a wrestler may submit by orating 'toe much'. Otherwise it's best of three legs (or toes, if you prefer), where wrestlers compete to pin their opponent's feet toe the ground (sorry) – this manoeuvre being termed a 'toe down'. Players must keep their non-wrestling foot airborne throughout, while their bottom and both palms must steadfastly remain on the ground for the bout's duration. Judges are positioned to check.

Celebrity status has been bestowed upon some top toe wrestlers, with Alan 'Nasty' Nash being flown to the US to appear on the *Jay Leno Show*. Tip-toeing towards the mainstream, the sport even featured in a question on *University Challenge* in 2011 when Clare College, Cambridge, failed to identify the Toe Wrestling World Championship – much to the inescapable irascibility of Jeremy Paxman.

A separate Women's World Championship title has been contested since 1999, displaying a healthy gender inclusivity towards appalling puns: the title twice being claimed by Na-toe-le Cartwright. Come on, it's enjoyable that the puns induce equivalent toe-curling to the wrestling itself. Contest tradition decrees that there's a pun orthodoxy, helping to emphasise the good-humoured element to this uniquely entertaining world championship. Maintaining the bad pun tradition was triumphant 2011 world champion The One and Only Preditoe (opposite).

Tortoise Racing

And they're off. I said, they're off! THEY'RE OFF!! That means start racing. Oh God, this happened last year too.

It's the annual Tortoise Race. Surrounded by an alluring circle of lettuce, tortoises representing several colleges are placed in the centre of an arena at Corpus Christi College, Oxford. There's not a hare in sight! Having witnessed last year's tortoise race, I'm forced to conclude that on this evidence, the tortoise must have got seriously lucky that famous day he triumphed over his big-eared leporine nemesis. Whereas a hare would, well, hare towards the food provided as a racing bribe, the tortoises initially seem remarkably uninterested.

A pretty undergraduate kisses the tortoise on his shell, and this has the effect – as it would on me – of merely sending him into an instant trance. Presumably having confirmed that he will not be turning into a handsome prince, she stops the kissing routine and releases him into the race. Nothing happens. The commentator, who is so 'Oxford' that the protagonists in *Brideshead Revisited* would give him a slap and order him to stop spouting such pompous grandiloquence, gamely fills in. Commentating on absolutely nothing is a decidedly difficult skill. Then the undergraduate girl's tortoise spurts forward, accelerating to a nausea-inducing speed; for fully two minutes he sprints forward, and then stops for a break after accomplishing 10cm.

Then nothing happens again.

There aren't many ninety-year-old world champions in sport, so take a (careful) bow Emmanuelle of Regent's College, Oxford. She must have enjoyed her winner's lap of honour (although, given she's a geriatric tortoise, it probably took 3 to 4 days).

Mirroring Olympic gender scandals, Emmanuelle was wrongly passed-off as male for several decades – when she answered (albeit very slowly) to Emanuel.

After dominating the race throughout the 1990s and the noughties, Emmanuelle was forced to be content with second place in 2010 when home tortoise Oldham won – but not before highlighting controversy that burned throughout the sport and singed its reputation – as Corpus's second tortoise (named Richard Fox after the college's 1517 founder) pushed several others out of the way, thus nobbling their chances. Controversy had also raged in 2009, when two amorous tortoises traded their chance of lettuce glory for opportunistic tortoise by coupling inches from the lettuce line, thus allowing Magdalen's tortoise Oscar to claim an improbable, if celibate, victory. A sportsman distracted by a sex scandal? That would never happen in the human world.

141

Underwater Hockey

Basically, this is ice hockey after a prolonged power cut. Sticks, pucks and players splash about, while spectators strain to obtain a view of the submerged action. Viewed through an aquatic filter of distortion, it is difficult to see the puck – both as a spectator and player – and hence any point. This is occasionally exploited by some players who pretend they are in possession of the puck, which draws incautious defenders towards them, leaving gaps to be exploited elsewhere by team-mates who have genuine puck custody.

Hitting the puck forward more than a few centimetres at a time proves immensely difficult. Hence players tend to hack away like a golfer stuck indefinitely in a bunker – only with water rather than sand constantly flying upwards and outwards while the puck remains stubbornly stationary.

In order to compare Underwater Hockey with its conventional sibling, I attend a field hockey match. My attention is drawn to a player isolated on the wing, disinterested in proceedings, walking up and down like a young William Wordsworth composing a sonnet. After 20 minutes displaying an utter disinclination to be involved with either the game or seemingly sports in general, a fiercely struck pass means he now has to make contact with his stick, or risk a bruised shin. He elects the former option, but it's clearly a late decision that could have gone either way. Then something genuinely remarkable happens. He drops his shoulders, and glides past a defender, then another. Tapping the ball in front, unafraid of relinquishing possession, he transforms into cheetah speed and reaches it ahead of a nearer opponent. Then another hip-swivelling dummy and four beaten opponents are left behind in dizzying, spinning confusion, either resignedly scratching their heads or laying prostrate on the turf, while he exploits the unguarded penalty area to find an unmarked striker who simply clips the ball into a yawning net. All his team-mates run over to embrace him, leaving the self-conscious scorer to receive no congratulations. Which, under the circumstance, was fair enough. It is a remarkable moment of out-of-context skill and fluidity, that sadly doesn't occur again. The game then returns to constant whistle fragmentation.

Underwater Hockey is a bit like the conventional hockey match, only without that good bit. It's not a spectator sport – mainly because everything takes place underwater. One player shouts rousingly to his team-mates – traceable only by a stream of bubbles rising to the surface – temporarily forgetting that he's underwater and so no one can hear him.

In conclusion, Underwater Hockey is one to play, not watch. Oh well, you have to try these things once.

Uppies & Downies

Famously, there are no rules for this ancient football game that has occurred for centuries in the Cumbrian town of Workington. Once a Football League side until the town vacated its League status to make room for Wimbledon in 1977, Workington has hosted Uppies & Downies football for considerably longer than the newer, modernistic and neoteric variant more familiar to today's sporting audience.

The town is divided into two bellicose halves, by a hatred presumably long since unfastened from whatever was the original reason (maybe someone said something slightly ambiguous about someone else's hat in 1563?). Geographical birthplace determines where players' loyalties lie; hence those born above the Cloffocks are Uppies, while those born down – OK you can probably work out how this sentence will finish. Uppies were traditionally coal miners, while Downies loaded iron ore onto boats. Throughout the nineteenth and early twentieth centuries, crowds approaching 30,000 were common. There was, of course, no television; people were happier then – there was no Piers Morgan.

Balls are constructed by local craftsmen from 2½ yards of leather, stuffed with wool; up until the 1920s, each match ball was routinely stuffed with horse hair, but wool was possibly the last concession made to modernity. The game is staged on three separate days each Easter. Goals are over a mile apart, with the Downies charged with resolutely defending a capstan at Workington harbour, while the Uppies aim to stop the Downies scoring a 'hail' in their goal: the park wall at ruined Workington Hall.

Deaths have been recorded – four in the modern era – but locals clearly consider the ultimate price a cheap commodity when it comes to defending some fellow locals from pointlessly lobbing a ball stuffed with wool through a piece of ruined park wall. But clearly I'm not from Workington. And it unmistakably does matter to the people of Workington – it's mattered since medieval times. In the 2006 game, the ball reached the town centre shops and screaming shoppers ran panicking for cover like a B-movie monster scene. Such scenes prompted the police to issue an official statement: 'we would ask players to think seriously about following the ball if it gets in to the building site, which has many hidden dangers.' That was it.

A man attired in an anachronistic blazer and purposefully clutching a clipboard replied to another elderly spectating gentleman's enquiry of 'how's it going?' with the unlikely response, 'the Uppies will be crucified today – quite literally.' Apparently that's not against the rules.

Workington, Ashbourne, Cornwall, Leicestershire, Lincolnshire and the Ba football games in Scotland are all relatively isolated communities. This partially explains their traditional football longevity, having successful reached the twenty-first century intact. Many other British towns and communities held their own long-standing ancient football games which have reverberated down the centuries with steadfastly upheld origins. But these games were virulently targeted by the authorities, who saw them as festivals of disorder and working class uncouthness; hence (at that time) Middlesex's Kingston upon Thames staged their last traditional town football game in 1868, after a campaign by the authorities that took fully seventy years to deliver its objective. Even polite and prosperous Dorking in Surrey had an annual game, but the authorities had successfully battled it out of existence by 1895 – although rendering it one of the longest survivors.

However, whereas kings, queens, prime ministers, invaders and changing fashions were powerless to stop the game, a far more powerful foe briefly threatened to end Workington's traditional game in 2009: namely Tesco. Plans to build a new supermarket on the Cloffocks rendered its future uncertain. Yet locals merely pledged to carry on playing around any new supermarket, and the game continues today – much to the dismay of the Uppies who endured a 0–3 humiliation in 2011, watched by nearly 500 smug Downies.

The 2011 game was notable for long periods of play spent scrapping in a scrapyard (seems appropriate), before 150 players entered the river (seems inappropriate). Pursuing the ball in the river is actually traditional, but the 2011 game saw forty players desperately jump from a railway bridge for a relatively sensible (in context) reason: a train was coming!

Britain is richer for Uppies & Downies existing (although the council may not be after the damage), with the good people of Workington nobly keeping this genuinely historical event alive.

Wife Carrying Race

eld each March on a Sunday morning in Dorking, the British Wife Carrying Race enables females, shackled by marriage and a determined avoidance of this modern fad of liberation, to be carried by their husbands over a 250-metre course in order to win beer. Whereas selecting a light wife would appear tactically expedient for racing, the prize is awarded in direct proportion to weight – so a slim petite waify wife (the 'I ate a radish two days ago and now I'm full' type) would

initially appear advantageous, though the victor would only win about the equivalent of eight cans of Stella. Work up a sweat humping a meatier wife up the undulating quarter of a kilometre course, and carrying the corpulent missus will reward the winner with considerably more beer (and recurring back problems). Clearly this is something to consider carefully before proposing.

Technically, and inclusively, participating couples can be of any gender, and need not necessarily carry their own wife. If you haven't had experience of picking up someone else's wife (i.e. you're not a Premiership footballer), then the required physical endurance of this event may be surprising – like many of the excellent events that the British excel at organising featured in this book, Wife Carrying Racing combines raising money for good causes with both fun and taxing athleticism.

The largest field in the event's four-year history contested the 2011 race, with 17 courageous runners and riders travelling the course of exactly 2 furlongs on good to soft ground. The event, after an enormous build-up following vast amounts of preparation and persuasion, proved to be over extremely quickly – under 2 minutes to be exact – inviting allegorical comparisons of matrimonial prematurity. The winning time of 1 minute 50 seconds was fractionally outside the record for a course that comes with obstacles: there's a 10-metre undulation and straw bale fences rise out of the ground like anti-tank defences. Time penalties are encountered for dropping a wife.

Although British couples traditionally dominate the rostrum positions in the Wife Carrying UK Championship, British upper lips and competition are both much stiffer when tackling the Wife Carrying World Championship. Staged annually in Sonkajärvi, Finland, the competition has yet to a produce a British winner: dominant Estonia (11 times winners) and Finland (4 times) have shared the last fifteen world titles between them. Whereas the British version is a pleasingly Middle England affair with politeness and flasks much in evidence alongside impressive athleticism and charity promotion, Finland brings somewhat more disturbing origins to their version, based on the legend of Herkko Rosvo-Ronkainen, an eighteenth-century forest dweller renowned for entering other villagers' log cabins and stealing their food and wives. If the people of eighteenth-century Finland residing in log cabins had the sense to fit locks,

then maybe they wouldn't dominate the sport today. Iceland are another world leader in the sport, possessing a particular and peculiar penchant for a wives carrying husbands race.

Equality is somewhat restored by the inhabitants of New South Wales who organise an annual Husband Dragging Race. Strict rules decree that the men must be prostrate and motionless (likely known as their default setting in Australia), while wives must clutch their ankles and drag husbands along a lubricated sheet for 200 metres. One recent winning wife called Shelia (yes, really) provided the following quote, 'I've never seen so much oil and mess on sheets before – at least not when my husband's around.' We like Shelia.

Woolsack Racing

etbury in Gloucestershire hosts an annual 240 yard race. Not that far, eh? Well, it requires a steep 1 in 4 uphill climb. Still mildly underwhelmed? Competitors must carry a huge voluminous bag weighing 60lbs. More impressed now, aren't you? The steepness of the hill, Gumstool Hill, cannot be downplayed. Racers must raise their game, woolsack and gaze at the starting line, and, seeing the demoralising ascent ahead, experience crushing inadequacy. This is quickly followed by the realisation that it's too late to pull out now – they've already paid their entrance fee. And besides, there are overseeing celebrities booked to attract glamour to the event.

Wool haulers who haven't taken what would have been an entirely natural decision to quit at the start, wear numbered bibs, and the prescribed technique is to carry the bales above their necks.

Woolsack Racing is commonly considered to have originated in the late seventeenth century as an attempt to impress local females. However, the event wasn't formalised until 1973, so it took just 300 years to get organised – well, you know what it's like when there's paperwork to find.

One competitor trips, prompting a spontaneous concerned gasp from the crowd; unfortunately he falls over during the fastest part of the circuit. Unlike

The World Famous Woolsack Races & Street Fair

Late May Bank Holiday Monday

Sponsored by THE SNOOTY FOX

a footballer, however, he's quickly back on his feet, swings the woolsack up off the ground and sets off with knees and ego only slightly grazed, applauded by the supportive crowd.

Tetbury occupies a strategically important position on the historical wool routes that originated in the Cotswolds; fleeces would be traversed east to London for sale and then on through the ports to Belgium and France where the wool spinners resided.

Men carry 60lbs of wool, while females are granted a concessionary 25lbs. The original course sensibly ran between two pubs: an accumulated distance of 280 yards, though this has been reduced in recent years to 240 yards. Wheelbarrows are not specifically mentioned in the rules, but a sharp-eyed vigilant official may attempt disqualification if spotted.

Although there are solo participants, the majority of entrants are teams of four, dividing the race into a four-person relay team. An approximate average time is 4–5 minutes to complete the course as a team, with the world record

(officially sanctioned by the *Guinness Book*) being 2 minutes 53 seconds accomplished in 1983. Mixed teams also participate, and sides can choose their team names; like pub quizzes, this results in inevitably laboured puns, arching the unoriginal, the witless and the actually-that's-quite-clever categories; positioned in the latter category was a mixed team christened Sack It And See.

World's Biggest Liar
CHAMPIONSHIPS

This competition (dis)honours a nineteenth-century landlord of the Bridge Inn where the competition is held in Santon Bridge in picturesque lakeland Cumbria. Yarn spinning on an industrial level awaits the curious visitor, as do tales of enormous owls and 6ft tall rabbits – although these need not necessarily be lies, given the venue's proximity to Sellafield nuclear power station.

Firstly, I'd counsel against taking home the offered prize money with anything but a pinch of salt equivalent to a leading crisp manufacturer's annual order. Billing yourself as the World's Biggest Liar Championship does rather insulate the organisers against disappointed winners being handed a free pint and £10 worth of vouchers for the pub's Sunday carvery, even if it does say 'winner will receive £10 million cash' on the chalkboard outside. It also proclaimed 'good value quality food', but they became distinctly prickly when I enquired if that was presumably another obvious lie too.

The event was started by a former landlord of the pub who regaled locals with stories theorising that the Lake District was not formed by volcanic activity, but by a large burrowing mole. Who liked giant turnips. In fact, one giant turnip was made into a cow shed. Hmmm. Comedic maestro Sue Perkins (sans Mel) took the 2006 title. Really, she did. Yes I do expect you to believe that. Her story foretold of a hole in the Ozone layer caused by flatulent Cumbrian sheep and their 'muttons of mass destruction'. Fibbers are permitted 5 minutes' stage time and strictly no props. Basically it's the country's largest collection of pathological liars residing under one roof (which is a suspiciously true fact, given the event is held in late November while the House of Commons is in recess).

Worm Charming
WORLD CHAMPIONSHIPS

I know, I know, having read this far, you've probably progressed way beyond incredulity, but this is a distinctly bizarre event. Having drawn lots to receive their plot, competitors have merely 30 frantic minutes to collect as many worms as they can, while abiding to rule number 4, 'Worms must not be dug'. In case you're wondering: vibrations can be used.

The 32nd championship took place in 2011 at the same location where the event started in 1980: Willaston near Nantwich in Cheshire – scene of a 531-worm haul by Mr Shufflebotham in the competition's inaugural contest. As the years turned into decades, worm charmers everywhere speculated on whether Mr Shufflebotham's total would ever be topped, and in 2009 it was finally eclipsed when a couple, only prepared to give their names as Mr and Miss Smith presented the judges with a catch of 567 worms. That, ladies and gentleman, provided another world record for Britain; in truth, it's probably a Willaston Record rather than a world record, yet since the organisers possess sufficient hubris to think global, we'll comply with their description: world record. Take that, China, USA and Germany.

Competition is tight, as are the outcomes: in 2003 the prescribed 30 minutes of worming culminated in a joint 167-worm tie between two competitors. Having consulted the rules – rule 17 – an additional 5-minute Worm-Off was ordered, resulting in one team collecting another 13 worms, while their opponents hauled into their plot pot an additional 14 worms – winning by the length of a single worm. Surely there are Hollywood movie rights forthcoming: suggested movie tagline: 'One man had worms'.

The worm charming area masquerades as a primary school playing field for the other less important 364 days of the year, before being catapulted into national limelight (a BBC crew were spotted). The Cheshire soil is densely populated with worms, and this particular part of the county is evidently the Hong Kong of the worm

world when it comes to population density. Competitors are allocated a 3x3-metre defined patch of ground in order to capture as many worms as they can.

The intention is to charm the worms into popping up to the surface for a curious glance of terra firma. Tapping the ground appears the most popular tactic, as does hitting various new age instruments. But all kinds of improvised charming techniques are in evidence. But beware: this does involve men in unflattering sandals strumming acoustic guitars.

While some rely on the dual-pronged charm offensive of tapping and strumming, empirical evidence proves that the most reliable technique is quadruple-pronged: literally, as it's a four-pronged fork which is pushed into the ground, and then hit to produce what are presumably waves of Beach Boys-like good vibrations, a strategy known by the colloquialism 'twanging'. Up the worms pop in their plots, and into the pots they plop (you probably want to avoid having to read that sentence out loud).

Roving officials are on the lookout for mendacity – crudely doubling your worm score with a sharp knife is rightfully frowned upon, as is arriving at the event carefully carrying several carrier bags emblazoned with the logo 'Bob's Bait Shop'.

Large worms are weighed, with the heaviest in the competition's history being a worm charmed by a Mr Oversall in 1987, weighing an impressive 6.6g; although at that weight, he may have bulked up his worm haul pot with a bemused grass snake.

More squeamish wormers are permitted to appoint a second to handle their worms (rule 11). Like other eccentric British sports responsible for enriching the vocabulary, this position has an official noun: a gillie.

And you have to say that Willaston takes its event seriously – the champion charmer receives a trophy modelled in the shape of a worm. Obvious, really. Oh, and there's an afternoon start time, so that 'early bird catches the worm' theory is rendered obsolete.

Acknowledgements

I'd like to thank all the kind people who helped with this project. As someone who cycles, I value this reconfirming validation of human kindness provided by those (many of them strangers) who have aided me – it offsets all that vexatious abuse shouted daily through wound-down car windows; although, on second thoughts, I may just be a very bad cyclist.

Enormous, container-sized thanks to the people who so kindly allowed me to feature their photographs, especially fundraiser extraordinaire Joel Hicks. Equally vast gratitude to the participants, organisers, spectators and volunteers who helped me with research and interviews. Special thanks to Andy Beal, Eamon Curry, Paul Harwood, Adam Hollier, Eric Meyer, Paul Norman, Nigel Perry, John Phipp, Lizzie Porter, Matt Stabeler, John P. Shearer, Dale Stephens, Roz South, Betty Stocker, Ben Ward, Tim Warnett, Pat Wood and Dean 'Zozman'.

Luxurious top-of-the-range thanks to Oliver Ledbury; I could have written this book and my newspaper column without Oliver's proofing skills and sagacity, but it wouldn't have been anything like as good; plus 'proofing' would probably be spelt with three o's. Prooof readding is nit my forty.

The kindness of all these people, coupled with the wonderful social cohesion evident in the colourful sports rightly celebrated here – albeit sports nobly upholding ancient traditions or inventing original eccentric pastimes – ensured writing this book helped bring me closer to Britain as a nation and a people (excluding shouty motorists). Thank you.

Celebrating Britain's most eccentric sports will hopefully help deliver Olympic recognition and inclusion; after all, one of the maddest sports I've ever witnessed is still the Skeleton Bob, and that delivered a bona fide Olympic gold medal for Amy Williams' perilous 80mph descent on a mouse mat.

Picture Credits

Alnwick Shrovetide Football – courtesy of paphotos.com
Aunt Sally – Richard O. Smith
Ba Game – John P. Shearer
Bar Billiards – Richard O. Smith
Black Pudding Throwing – Phil Taylor ARPS
Bognor Birdman – International Bognor Birdman http://www.birdman.org.uk; Holly Walsh courtesy of PBJ Management
Bottle-Kicking – Adam Hollier
Brambles Cricket – courtesy of paphotos.com
British Open Crabbing – p. 30 and inset p. 31 courtesy of David Leatherdale; p. 31 main courtesy of paphotos.com
Bumps Races – Wolfson & St Cross Boat Club
Cheese Rolling – courtesy of Jean Jefferies
Chess Boxing – courtesy of James Bartosik, http://bartosik.org
Clog Cobbing – courtesy of Joel Hicks, www.alwayswithasmile.com
Coal Carrying – courtesy of Joel Hicks, www.alwayswithasmile.com
Conkers World Championship – www.worldconkerchampionships.com
Crazy Golf World Championship – Richard O. Smith
Cross-Channel Swimming Race – courtesy of Dr Julie Bradshaw MBE, www.getset4success.co.uk
Custard Pie World Championship – P. 54 pics from Mike Fitzgerald; others courtesy of Joel Hicks, www.alwayswithasmile.com
Cycle Polo – http://www.bikepolo.org.uk/ & www.cycleoxford.coop
Dwile Flonking – Tim Warnett
Gravy Wrestling World Championship – courtesy of Joel Hicks, www.alwayswithasmile.com
Great Knaresborough Bed Race – Nigel Perry
Great Shirt Race – Dale Stephens
Gurning World Championship – Betty Stocker www.bettystocker.com
Haxey Hood – Dean 'Zozman'
Horseball – http://british-horseball-association.btck.co.uk/
Korfball – Fo Krabben/Didcot Dragons
Lawnmower Racing – Richard O. Smith
Men's Netball – Andy Dawson

Monopoly World Championships – Richard O. Smith
Mountain Bike Chariot World Championships – courtesy of Joel Hicks, www.alwayswithasmile.com
Nettle Eating World Championships – © Jonathan Tolhurst
Onion Eating World Championship – Richard O. Smith
Pantomime Horse Grand National – Thomas Vale Construction
Pea Shooting World Championships – www.witcham.org.uk
Pea Throwing World Championship – Roz South www.allthingsbrightonbeautiful.com
Pie Eating World Championship – Iain Macauley www.pressrelations.co.uk
Pooh Sticks World Championship – http://www.pooh-sticks.com/
Pram Racing – Matt Stabeler http://oldtowncarnivalweek.co.uk/
Real Tennis – http://www.outc.org.uk/
Royal Shrovetide Football – Eamon Curry
Scrabble British Championship – Richard O. Smith
Shin Kicking Championships – Betty Stocker www.bettystocker.com
Snail Racing World Championship – Mark Scase
Stilton Cheese Rolling World Championship – www.ecofocus.co.uk
Stone Skimming World Championships – © Laura McMahon
Tar Barrels – http://www.otterytarbarrels.co.uk/
Tiddlywinks – ETwA
Tin Bath World Championships – John Phipp
Toad in the Hole – Ben Ward
Toe Wrestling World Championship – http://www.bentleybrookinn.co.uk
Tortoise Racing – Eric Meyer & the *Oxford Student*
Underwater Hockey – courtesy of paphotos.com
Uppies & Downies – Pat Wood
Wife Carrying Race – www.trionium.com
Woolsack Racing – courtesy of Joel Hicks, www.alwayswithasmile.com
World's Biggest Liar Championships – Jennings Brewery
Worm Charming World Championships – courtesy of Peter King